~ Scrambled Eggs ~
~ Walking on Shells ~

By Olivia Valency

ISBN: 979-8-9946200-8-3

Any mention of Calvinism is specific to the church where I grew up and how I recall it being taught to me by my mom, teachers, and preachers throughout my life. It's not always taught the same way in all Calvinist churches.

For privacy reasons, some names, locations, and dates may have been changed.

First edition, March 2026

Books written by Olivia Valency

Scrambled Eggs ~ Walking on Shells

Sunny Side Up ~ Eggshells to Seashells

Deviled Eggs ~ Shells in the Yolk

Poached Eggs ~ Selling Empty Shells

Over Easy ~ Cracking the Shell

Special thanks to my daughters,
Hannah and Heather,
for proofreading and editing.

TABLE OF CONTENTS

~ Rotten Roosters ~

Badgers are terrifying and vicious animals when cornered. My dad's demeanor was like that of a cornered badger. He was a ferocious and cantankerous man. Badger was the nickname we all called him behind his back. He was gross, perverted, vulgar, crude, and abusive. His heart was murderous and dark.

Dad often lost his temper. It was an awful sight watching him gnash his teeth and snarl. He was always cursing us out. We were in constant fear. Anyone getting close to him risked being hit, kicked, or cursed at. Every single day, he threatened our lives. The extreme abuse he inflicted will haunt us until we die. Nobody ever forgets meeting him. It's an awkward encounter. Seriously, he was a person you never forgot.

I can only speculate about how he became such a terrible person. I gathered some bits of information from my mom and my oldest sister, Anna. His parents and siblings likely instilled this menacing behavior in him. Dad was the youngest in his family. Often, the baby gets spoiled rotten. Many times, spoiled children grow up to be rotten adults.

My dad's parents, Albert and Lucille, died before I was born. They had 11 children — six girls and five boys. Dad's brothers, sisters, and their spouses have also passed away.

There's nobody left to ask how he became a horrifying monster.

Dad's grandparents came to the U.S. from Sweden in the 1800s. They were tall, with fair hair and blue eyes. Around the same time, his mom's parents moved here from Germany. They had dark hair and brown eyes. Sweden and Germany both have cold winters and scorching summers. My ancestors likely believed they could handle the northern Midwestern climate of the United States, as it is similar to what they were used to.

Winters in the northern states of America can be severe. Temperatures can drop to as low as -25°F. Surprisingly, the wind chill can often make it feel like -50°F or colder. Summers are also extremely hot. Temperatures reach up to 105°F. Corn is the main crop there. One acre can transpire four thousand gallons of water daily. This makes the humidity unbearable.

Cornfields surrounded the chicken farm where I grew up. While we worked on the farm, we used 5-gallon buckets to carry water and food to all our various farm animals. While working in that intense heat and humidity, it felt as if the sweat dripping from our bodies could have filled both buckets. During those hot summer months, you would hear us say, "Argh, I've been sweatin' buckets out there!"

My ancestors were farmers. The men worked on the farms, and their wives were mothers and homemakers. Living through these two extreme temperatures year round can push farmers and their families to their physical and mental limits. Not only are they burdened with daily tasks, but also with severe weather.

Lured by promises of cheap land, Dad's grandparents migrated to this harsh northern climate. Farming and growing crops had likely been their trades in Sweden and Germany. They were searching for a location where they could use their skills. The fertile black soil may have enticed them.

I was eventually born into this freezing and unbearably hot environment. Nobody in their right mind should choose a place where temperatures and wind chills drop below zero for seven long, miserable months. My ancestors never got the memo that birds migrate south during the winter.

Many people up north experience seasonal depression. Winters are bitter, cold, long, dark, and gloomy. Families are all cooped up together indoors. They don't get enough sunlight. They often become irritable and grouchy. As the months grow longer, everyone gets on each other's nerves. If it's an abusive home, there's nowhere to escape, and depression sets in even deeper.

Midwesterners speak fast and are straightforward. Working outside in extreme weather can make some people irritable, impatient, and demanding. They prefer not to be outside longer than necessary. They wish to be understood the first time they say something. It's unbearable outside, and they don't want to repeat themselves. You won't find them standing outside chatting. They want to finish the outdoor chores quickly so they can get back inside.

Many farmers had large families. They felt proud when their wives gave birth to a son. They would strut around town like *roosters* with their chests puffed out. The boys worked outside with their dad. The girls helped their mom with caring for the children, doing laundry, cooking, cleaning, and gardening. Most farmers got excited about a baby boy because it meant more help on the farm. It also meant they could pass their farm and last name on to the next generation.

Back then, farmers took pride in their last names. The oldest boy was the heir. If he passed away, the inheritance went to the second-oldest son. Many men gave their firstborn boys the same first name. The father was called Senior, and his son was called Junior.

The girls were never heirs to the property unless there was no living son. When girls married, they changed their last names to their husbands'. The men didn't want their farm to be inherited by someone outside the family.

Men "wore the pants" in the home. He provided the money and the roost. He was the head of the household. This worked well if he was hardworking, responsible, faithful, loving, and had common sense. If he was abusive, lazy, irresponsible, unfaithful, selfish, arrogant, or lacked common sense, it didn't work out so well.

Many abusive men weren't interested in girl babies. They saw them as liabilities, weak and useless. Some turned up their noses when they heard their baby was a girl. They showed great disrespect toward women. They berated them, calling them weak and telling them to keep their place. The place they spoke of was for her to be his servant. She was to care for the children, clean, garden, cook, do laundry, and be intimate with him as often as he demanded. He wore the big boy, King Tut pants. The woman was to be at his beck and call.

The abusive master referred to his wife as "that female" or "the old lady." He wanted everyone to understand she was his lesser half. He called girls "heifers," referring to them as cows. Some of the verbally abusive men also physically abused their families.

Women could not voice their opinions at home or in church. They were to stay quiet. Mister Head Honcho would decide for his family. His word was final. He saw himself as the god of his house and expected everyone to bow down to him. He was the supreme boss. Anyone who dared to contradict him would face his wrath. He demanded respect as he was the *rooster* who ruled the roost.

~ Mother Hens ~

Women felt grateful if their firstborn child was a girl. That meant they would have a second little *mother hen* to help with household chores and care for future children. Mothers and daughters in large families were like workhorses. It was their job to feed, clean up after, dote on, and cater to the dad and boys.

Albert and Lucille had a large family that required a whirlwind of daily chores. Caring for many children was exhausting. Mothers needed someone to watch the babies while they managed their endless workload.

Dad's oldest sister, Edna, became the second *mother hen* in their family. It was her job to keep her younger siblings fed, quiet, and happy. It was also her responsibility to make sure everyone completed their chores correctly and on time. Many of the children resented their sister for telling them what to do. They often became rebellious toward her. You could hear them shouting, "You can't tell me what to do! You're not my mom!"

Lucille was 44 when she had my dad and his twin sister, Sophia. The babies were likely a surprise. They arrived eight years after her other nine older children. My aunt Diana was 8 years old. She became a secondary *mother hen* to these two real baby dolls.

From what I've heard, Edna and Diana spoiled them rotten. They never told the kids no. Dad learned that throwing temper tantrums got him what he wanted. He screamed, yelled, cried, bit, and hit. His *mother hens* gave in to his every whim to keep him quiet. They would do anything to avoid his anger, screaming, and temper tantrums.

If Sophia got a new toy, Dad also wanted one. Anytime his siblings received something new, he threw a fit. When Lucille made Sophia a dress, he demanded to have one too. He was a rotten brat!

If a boy wore dresses or played with dolls, family members would mock and tease him. They called him a sissy. Dresses and dolls were only for girls. Boys were told to go outside and play in the dirt with toy cars, tractors, and dump trucks. Mom's sent them to help their dad or brothers in the garage or on the farm.

For any mother, at any age, having one baby is overwhelming. Babies require a tremendous amount of work. Lucille, unexpectedly having twins later in her life, added much additional stress.

The twins were 8 years old when World War II began. It was a tough time for farmers. They faced labor shortages because their sons and hired help were being drafted into the military. Factories also struggled to find workers because many employees were called to serve in the war. Many left the farms for work in the factories and war production plants. Those jobs paid better than what farmers could offer.

Farmers put their wives and younger children to work. The war increased the demand for food, so farmers had to double their production. Farmers' wives and daughters now had twice the work to do.

Lucille died at 58 years old. The twins were 14. Healthcare wasn't easily accessible, and doctor visits were too costly for large families. Mothers were often the last to get care for their own health issues. Their primary focus was on providing food for their children. They wouldn't spend money on doctor visits or new clothes for themselves.

Dad never talked about his childhood, so I can only guess why or how his mom died so young. It may have been genetic. Extreme weather, high stress levels, and intense physical labor might have shortened her lifespan.

Lucille might have been sick. A sickly mother would be lenient. She would have given the kids whatever they wanted to keep them quiet. Edna would have understood Lucille's condition well. She would have spoiled the twins to make life less stressful for her mother.

Abused children often become abusers themselves or marry someone who is an abuser. Abuse is all they've known. It's what feels normal to them. A child raised in an abusive home rarely receives genuine love from their parents and siblings. If someone shows them genuine love and affection, it often feels unfamiliar, uncomfortable, and frightening. They might think the person is fake. They don't know how to respond, and they want to run away from it.

Loving behavior feels odd to them, so they find a partner who displays the same abusive behavior they experienced during childhood. That's comfortable, and they see harmful actions as normal. Physical, emotional, sexual, and verbal abuse, along with anger, vulgarity, and perversion, are all they know. It's all they've seen, and it's what they've sadly become accustomed to.

There's a strong possibility that Albert was abusive. My dad didn't turn into this angry monster one day out of the blue. After witnessing Dad's murderous nature, I can imagine there might have been foul play involved in Lucille's death. I have found no record of her death date nor an obituary. For all I know, they may have dug a hole and buried her in their backyard.

Lucille may also have unintentionally abused her children. Like many battered wives, she would have withdrawn into survival mode. In that state, she would have neglected the children's emotional needs as she struggled to survive in an inescapable, abusive marriage.

Edna would have stepped in as the mother hen. She would have spoiled the twins rotten as she took them under her wing to protect them. Edna likely prevented physical harm to them. However, she wouldn't have covered their eyes and ears. They would have seen and heard the tumultuous, vulgar, and abusive people around them.

Many church leaders didn't allow divorce. Women couldn't escape the abusive situations that trapped them. Even if churches had permitted divorce, mothers couldn't support all those children on their own. Feeling stuck, they yearned for the day their nightmare would end. They trudged through life with a heavy burden on their shoulders. Constantly feeling pain in their battered and broken hearts, they daydreamed about having wings to fly away.

~ Early Birds ~

Albert and Lucille may both have grown up in abusive homes. Besides Lucille's seemingly early death, when I looked back into my ancestry, I noticed some other strange, unexplained early deaths.

Lucille's father, my great-grandfather Ernie, was married to his first wife, Lillith, for 12 years. They had six children, including twin baby girls who mysteriously died the same year they were born. Daisy was premature and died at birth. Eliza Jane was born 12 days after Daisy. She passed away at five months old.

Five years later, Lillith also had an early death at age 31. These three unexplained deaths remain a mystery. I haven't been able to find an obituary for Lillith or her babies. I found a church bulletin notice where Ernie said that Lillith had died from a quick consumption, meaning she died of a fast-acting tuberculosis. Tuberculosis isn't a fast death. I immediately sensed a cover-up of something more horrifying.

I initially thought that Ernie had caused Lillith's death and had lied about it. Lillith may have been at church last Sunday. Now, this Sunday, she's dead. Ernie had to come up with a semi-believable reason for her death.

A year after Lillith died, Ernie married his second wife, my great-grandmother Martha. They were married in April, and my grandmother, Lucille, was born in October, just six months after their wedding. Martha had gotten pregnant with Ernie's baby sometime around Christmas. I'm not sure if Lillith's body was cold yet. However, Ernie was making babies with Martha just 10 months after Lillith's death.

Ernie, being so quick to have babies, made me wonder if he had been having an affair while Lillith was alive. Lillith was likely suffering from depression because her twin babies died. All mothers who lose a child become grief-stricken, depressed, and emotionally and romantically unavailable.

If Lillith had caught Ernie cheating, the heartbreak would have been unbearable. She may have taken her own life. However, she had four young children depending on her. It's more likely that Ernie beat her during an argument.

Rage was my dad's middle name. We are all lucky to be alive. We were always running from his fists of death. When he couldn't catch us, he always said, "You have to sleep sometime!" Many abusive men see themselves as the *rooster* that rules the roost. They rule their family through anger and rage. It's possible Ernie had this same rage.

I also pondered whether Ernie was involved in the early deaths of their babies. He may have abused Lillith while pregnant. This would have led to her delivering the twins prematurely.

Our ancestors, both men and women, treated children born from premarital relationships harshly. They labeled them as illegitimate or bastards. Community and church members would mutter these insults and joke about them during coffee gatherings and beer-drinking parties.

They were also judgmental and critical toward the girl who became pregnant before marriage. For years, like *hens* pecking and scratching, they shunned her as they made snide comments about her.

Ernie's second wife, Martha, would have panicked when she realized she was pregnant. She likely felt scared and alone, with no one to talk to. She couldn't let her family, church, and community know she had gotten pregnant before marriage. They would scorn and shame her. She didn't want everyone calling her baby cruel names.

To hide her pregnancy, Martha likely devised a plan to marry Ernie quickly. They likely married fast by going to the judge at the courthouse. Back then, a quick marriage because of an unplanned pregnancy was commonly called a shotgun wedding.

The phrase ‘shotgun wedding' describes a hasty marriage where the pregnant girl's father insists that the man marry his daughter to care for her and the baby. Sometimes, the girl's father brought his shotgun along. Our ancestors held a "you play — you pay" attitude toward premarital pregnancies.

Sometimes, a girl and a boy lived together without being married. People told the boy he needed to make her an honest woman. They weren't suggesting that the girl was dishonest; they meant the boy should marry her so she would be a respectable woman. They viewed unmarried couples living together as living in sin.

Martha didn't truly know Ernie. In her panic, she couldn't consider whether Ernie was the right person for her. She had no more time to find her Prince Charming.

She knew the gossipy *hens* in her town would count the months from her marriage to the birth of her little *early bird.* There would be rumors about her shotgun wedding. She hoped they wouldn't notice she was a few months short of the normal nine-month pregnancy. They always kept track. She often heard whispers about the bun coming out of the oven too soon. When Lucille was born, Martha likely said she was premature. She didn't realize this was the oldest trick in the book.

Parents rarely discussed the birds and the bees with their children. They feared it might spark their curiosity and lead to early romantic relationships. Birth control wasn't available until 1960. Many girls got pregnant and hastily married the father before finding a compatible partner.

The girls thought it was better to marry the baby's father quickly rather than to suffer scorn from their family, church, and community. Many jumped from the frying pan into the fire, as they entered a lifetime of living hell with an incompatible, abusive husband.

During marriage, many abusive men used this early pregnancy secret to control their wives. During an argument, he threatened to reveal her secret. It subdued her because she wanted to avoid shame and judgment. Besides, she would not let her child suffer from cruel name-calling. Men didn't want the secret exposed either, as he knew others would gossip about him. However, that didn't stop him from using it to wield power over his wife.

Many people were hypocritical in their shunning. As they sat around sipping their coffee or drinking their beers, they pretended they had never done such an ungodly thing. Most engaged in premarital intimacy themselves as teenagers.

Some got lucky, not getting pregnant. However, my family history shows that many of them did and covered it up. They too, hastily got married and claimed that their baby was premature and arrived early.

After their hasty marriage, Martha became stepmother to Ernie and Lillith's four children. Taking on four children who weren't her own was a massive responsibility. She probably wouldn't have if she hadn't felt the need to hide her pregnancy.

I found an old newspaper article about a Sunday afternoon beer party at Ernie's house. The party had lots of food and beer. Some guys were in the house playing cards. Others were outside playing games, racing horses, and betting money on who could kick the highest. A fight broke out, and one guy pulled out his pistol. He shot and killed the fellow who was trying to break up the fight. Alcohol, guns, and King Tut pants never turn out well for these *rotten roosters.*

After 16 years of marriage to Ernie, Martha also had an early death at the young age of 40. Lucille was 16 and had to finish raising her two sisters, Hattie, 14, and Carol, 12. I found no record of Martha's death. Again, I wondered if Ernie was involved in her death. Had she died of a fast-acting tuberculosis as well? I noticed a pattern of early deaths among the people surrounding Ernie. Martha lived a few years longer than Lillith, who mysteriously died at age 31.

~ Fresh Meat ~

Edna, was 33, unmarried, and still living at home when Lucille died. Edna had to finish raising the twins. Two children had moved out. Dad and Sophia were 14 years old. The other seven kids were all in their 20s or early 30s.

It was common for children to stay at home until they married. There was no stigma saying they had to move out at 18. Sometimes, children left home when they got married, and sometimes they didn't. Often, they would bring their new wives into the home and raise their children there. Other times, they built a small house on the property. Families stayed close in those days.

Most of my dad's siblings didn't get married at a young age. They all might have had his same angry, abusive attitude. It may have been difficult to find a spouse willing to marry someone so mean.

With the world in shambles, they may have wanted to stick together. Wars increase the cost of groceries, goods, and living expenses. Many children couldn't afford to leave home. My dad's parents were likely poor. The children likely felt obligated to stay and help their parents financially.

Albert and Lucille might have kept their family isolated. They probably wanted the kids at home to have more workers on their farm. If they had kept the children isolated, it would have been difficult for them to find a spouse.

There was sexual abuse in my childhood home, so Dad likely experienced the same in his. He learned his vulgar and perverse behavior from someone. It's likely Albert was sexually abusive and taught his boys to act that way too.

It wouldn't surprise me if I found out that Albert abused Edna. This may have led to the birth of the twins. Edna was 19 when they were born. It would also explain why she was still at home at 33 years old. It would also make sense why she spoiled the kids rotten.

There's an eight-year gap between Diana's birth and the babies. Birth control wasn't available, so Lucille either went through early menopause at age 38, or she had stopped sleeping with Albert. Many abused wives grow to hate their husbands. They sleep elsewhere. This often causes the abuser to escalate to a higher level of frustrated rage.

Albert may have killed Lucille during one of his angry outbursts. I couldn't shake the strange feeling in my stomach telling me Albert might have buried Lucille in their backyard. A death caused by rage and a quick backyard burial weren't uncommon back in the old days. Unless I find an obituary, I'll assume foul play was involved.

After Lucille's death, Diana, then 21, moved out and ended up in Nevada. There she met Gerald, a 40-year-old man. Diana soon became pregnant with her little *early bird,* Oscar. She quickly married Gerald to avoid shame and condemnation.

I wondered what drew Diana to someone 19 years older. Often, girls marry an older man if they have been powerless against their father. If someone had sexually abused her, she would have matured early. Her abuser robbed her of her childhood. Outsiders saw her as responsible and mature.

Boys of her age would have seemed immature. Diana would have needed someone older to match her level of maturity. When Gerald showed romantic interest, Diana may have thought it was love. Then, after getting pregnant, she likely felt she had to marry him to avoid shame from others.

Diana became a stepmother to Gerald's four teenage daughters. His oldest daughter, Lucy, was 15, only six years younger than Diana. She shared a similar name with Diana's mother. If Diana had been whimsical, she might have seen this as destiny.

Gerald had more life experience than Diana. He became wise in the ways of big-city life. He was a smooth talker. Diana was a naïve, sheltered farm girl whose mother had just died. She was fresh out in the world.

Gerald had been married twice before marrying my Aunt Diana. When he was 19, he married Marlene, a 13-year-old girl who was young and fresh. For an unknown reason, they annulled their marriage. They had a child together. Clarence followed in his father's footsteps. He was a meat cutter and worked in the meat processing industry for 60 years.

At age 24, Gerald married Elaine, who was 15 years old. She was nine years younger than Gerald. They had four daughters before they divorced. Gerald was marrying very young girls. Abuse and concern for her daughter's safety most likely prompted Elaine to divorce Gerald.

Three years after Oscar was born, Gerald and Diana moved to Idaho. Gerald grew up there, and his family still lived in the area. Around the same time, my dad's whole family packed everything up and moved close to Diana.

Diana was probably in serious trouble. She was likely being abused by Gerald. Dad's family would have wanted to help. They would put Gerald in his place. It was common for families to take it personally if someone outside the family hurt one of their daughters or sisters. It didn't matter if family members hurt each other — that wasn't as serious. However, an outsider harming a family member would have allowed them to prove how tough they were.

They may have moved there to show their presence to Gerald. If a good ol' boy talkin' to didn't work, then another good ol' boy friendly backyard burial would be in order.

But, lo and behold, wouldn't ya know, 10 months after moving, Diana died. Someone stabbed her through the throat with a razor-sharp boning knife. Gerald said he was hanging clothes on the clothesline. He said that when he returned to the house, he discovered Diana on the bathroom floor. The police found the knife under Diana's body.

Oscar was 4 years old. Diana had just given birth to a baby girl. Betsy was only 6 days old on the day of Diana's horrific death. Gerald told the officer that Diana had taken her own life. He also said she had been experiencing depression since giving birth. The police report concluded that Gerald used to be a *fresh-meat* butcher.

It's unheard of for a woman to stab herself this way. For crying out loud! No brand-new mother of a 6-day-old baby takes their own life. A stabbing in the throat is a "shut up" action from an external aggressor. Seeing a man hanging up clothes was also a rare sight. Doing laundry was women's work. Men didn't touch laundry — unless they needed an alibi for murder!

Severe postpartum depression leading a mother to take her own life six days after childbirth is rare. Childbirth depression doesn't develop so fast that a woman would take such drastic action this soon after giving birth unless she is psychotic.

There were no arrests in Diana's murder. However, you can bet yer boots I don't believe for one second that Diana took her own life. Nope! You can't pull the wool over my eyes. I'm 99.9% sure she was murdered — murdered by a *fresh-meat* butcher who had a sick, twisted mind toward fresh young girls.

~ Ruffled Feathers ~

If by some tiny chance Gerald didn't kill Diana, another strong possibility is that my dad did it. I have first-hand experience that he was capable of murder. His *feathers got ruffled* easily. In a split second, he went from calm to a ferocious rage.

Dad was used to getting all of Diana's attention. Her leaving home would have made him feel abandoned, furious, and jealous. Her abandonment would have been enough to make him stab her in the throat during a heated argument.

Whenever Dad had one of his rage episodes, he grabbed the first weapon he saw and threw it as hard as he could at whichever child had caused his anger. From an early age, we learned to dodge all the crazy flying objects. We became attuned to his moods and could tell instantly when his mood shifted for the worse. We were always on high alert and in self-protection mode. The next moment could mean we had to hide.

Knives were his favorite weapon. He always threatened that he was going to run us through with it. In one of his rage episodes, he cut my mom. She was using a knife at the kitchen counter when he blew into a tantrum. As she tried to ward him off, he shoved it at her, and it sliced a deep cut across her hand. Blood was gushing so severely that she had to get stitches.

After that day, when he had a rage episode, I instinctively moved to stand guard in front of the knife drawer. I hoped that if he didn't see it, he wouldn't think about using a knife. We could survive if he couldn't get to the knives or the guns.

After Aunt Diana's death, a few of my dad's siblings moved back to Wyoming. Now that she was gone, they returned home and resumed their lives. Albert and five of my dad's sisters stayed in Idaho. Dad ran off and joined the military.

He may have been running away from the murder of his sister. When someone commits an act of violence, murder, or an illegal act, they become afraid of getting caught. They try to run to a different state or country. In my mind, Dad remains a suspect in the death of his *mother hen.*

Dad didn't stay in the military long. They discharged him for an unknown medical reason. Likely, they didn't want someone with rage. He would've gotten everyone around him killed. There are some men you can trust with your life. Others are my dad-type, who you don't want around you when your life is at stake.

After discharge, Dad moved back to Wyoming to be near his brothers. They had all grown to hate each other and often fought fiercely. However, they were his family, and he felt compelled to be close to them.

Growing up, our family sometimes packed into our big station wagon to visit my dad's siblings. These gatherings were a huge disaster. Dad and his brothers often argued over trivial things. They yelled, shouted, and even got into fistfights. They accused Dad of lying and kept demanding he give their guns back, saying Dad had stolen them.

It was always a frightening visit. I tried to stay away from the yelling. However, I couldn't get far enough away. I felt ashamed that my dad lost control at other people's houses. It was normal for him to act angry in our home. However, his acting like this in public made me want to crawl into a hole and never come out.

Their fighting and arguing always ended with our leaving abruptly. The 30-minute ride back home felt treacherous. Dad remained furious and fuming throughout the entire drive home. Many times, we came close to having an accident. Nobody wore seat belts back then. We are all lucky to be alive.

Seeing those brothers fight so fiercely as adults, I assume they argued just as much growing up. I'm sure it was a chaotic mess, judging by the chaos Dad brought into my childhood home. He was a *rotten rooster* whose *feathers* always got *ruffled.*

People believed that blood is thicker than water. They believed that through thick and thin, families stick together. They didn't realize that blood means nothing when it comes to protecting ourselves from abusive people. Many felt obligated to put up with them because they had the same parents.

During those family gatherings, to avoid upsetting anyone, they never openly discussed Diana's death. Still, there were some quiet, hush-hush kitchen conversations. Dad's siblings believed Gerald had killed Diana.

Twice, we went to the cemetery to honor our deceased relatives. There was some secretive mention of something fishy surrounding my dad's grandfather, Ernie. They had suspicions about the early deaths of Martha, Lillith, and the two babies. They believed Ernie had done it.

~ Peach Pie ~

After returning home, Dad rented a room in the same house where my mom's sister, Dorothy, and her husband, Bob, lived. He was 24 when he moved in. Soon after, my mom, age 17, went to visit Dorothy. There she met my dad.

He completely fooled Mom, as he presented himself as Prince Charming. Portraying himself as the best thing since the invention of *peach pie,* he smeared his honey and peach jam on her naive and unsuspecting toast. As he lavished her with his sweet talk, my mom's heart flipped and flopped into what she thought was true love. Mom had no experience with boys. She had gone on a few dates after Thursday evening church classes. However, she wasn't prepared to handle a man much older than herself, who used fakery to swoon women. Mom didn't know such trickery existed.

My mom's parents, Bill and Harriet, weren't happy when my mom started dating him. They saw that his pie had a few holes in its crust. He was only pretending that he was the sweetest man ever.

My grandparents tried to discourage Mom from dating my dad. He attended a Lutheran church and held different religious beliefs. Mom's parents were born into a branch of Calvinism. They believed their church was the only one that had God's truth. They considered anyone who wasn't a member of their church to be a Gentile. The church discouraged mixing with or dating Gentiles.

Bill and Harriet weren't emotionally available or affectionate. Harriet had always been sickly. She experienced frequent dizzy spells and often needed to sit to keep her head from spinning. Besides that, their son James had recently died in a car accident. They were likely still grieving their loss.

Mom was the youngest in her family. Her parents were about to be empty nesters. They had recently lost James, and now their baby girl was dating a *peach pie* man who didn't have a holy crust. Their heartache was too much to bear. They didn't support my mom's decision. However, that didn't stop her from falling head over heels into what she thought was love.

Mom grew up in a sheltered home. Her parents were religious and kept her in a box to protect her from the outside world. She was just peeking out of that box when my dad smeared on his peach jam. She was naïve and fell hook, line, and sinker.

They had only been dating a short time when my mom got pregnant. She was panic-stricken! Nobody could find out! She had to cover this up fast. What to do, what to do! The church would make her stand up in front of the entire congregation to confess her guilt, shame, and sorrow. If her mom and dad found out, she would have to face their disappointment for bringing shame to the family.

Mom had no one to talk to. Sharing her secret with one person would put her at risk. Everyone would criticize, judge, and look down on her. She would be the subject of gossip until the day she died.

The only way to hide her pregnancy was to marry quickly. She thought that if she married now, she could still have her baby close to nine months later. No one would find out. If anyone questioned her, she would tell them it was premature and had arrived early. Yes, a quick marriage was best.

In her panic, in her fear, and in what must have been rivers of tears, Mom hurriedly made plans to get married at the courthouse. They asked Dad's brother, Richard, and his wife to be their witnesses. I'm sure she said nothing about the pregnancy. As soon as Mom signed the marriage papers, she felt an enormous sense of relief. She was now legally married. The only thing left was to announce her pregnancy — which she did one month later.

~ The Frying Pan ~

Mom's relief was only fleeting, as Dad showed his true nature. Her quick cover-up to dodge the outsiders gossiping about her instead trapped her in a different hell. As she tried to escape the condemnation of her church, she jumped from the *frying pan* into the fire.

Early on, they visited one of his brothers. The visit ended with their fighting over a lunchbox. They argued about who it belonged to. The argument grew so intense that they started fist-fighting. My dad likely stole it from him and lied so he could keep it.

Feeling appalled, Mom stepped in between them. He pushed her out of the way. There was nothing she could do to calm his rage. The more she tried, the angrier he became. She didn't know how to deal with people who fought, as she had grown up in a peaceful home. She had gotten herself into a pickle and was feeling the heat of her *frying pan.*

Mom's heart sank when she realized her new husband had a crush on one of his brother's daughters. He swooned over and flirted with Paula. It made my mom feel uncomfortable and leery of the man she married. He broke Mom's trust, and her heart began to crack.

In the same year, Albert passed away. My parents drove their new car to Idaho for the funeral. Two of Dad's brothers went with them. All three men took turns driving. The trip was terrible. All three brothers argued the entire way. Dad was very protective of his new car. It was foggy during the drive, and Dad fumed the whole time about how his brothers were driving.

After arriving in Idaho, Dad abandoned my mom for the entire few days they were there. He went to hang out with his twin sister, Sophia. Mom didn't know anyone. Horror and fear overtook her as she sat scared and alone. She spent the entire trip crying. Her heart sank as she realized she had married a monster. She felt an overwhelming sense of dread as she saw herself in a very hot *frying pan* that she could not escape.

Harriet also died that year at age 57. A year later, Bill remarried but died of a heart attack at age 65, one year after that.

When my parents first married, they lived in a one-bedroom apartment. Mom gave birth to Anna while living there. She tried to breastfeed, but she gave up because Anna was sleeping so much. Besides, Dad was making weird comments to her. Whenever he saw Mom being affectionate to Anna, he got jealous and demanded affection for himself as well. He didn't want to share Mom's attention with anyone. He was worse than a *rooster* that wouldn't let his *hen* sit on her eggs.

Mom soon became pregnant with her second baby. My parents moved into a small one-bedroom house, where Ella was born. The baby formula upset her stomach, causing terrible gas, and she was fussy most of the time. Ella cried and cried because her little stomach hurt so badly.

Dad couldn't cope with the non-stop sound of a crying baby. It drove him insane. He stormed angrily over to Ella, yanked her out of her crib, and shook her violently. Sometimes, he squeezed her tightly against his chest, trying to push the gas out of her stomach.

I'm shocked that Ella survived. She probably suffered from shaken-baby syndrome. If Ella, now an adult, had X-rays taken, they would likely reveal broken ribs from childhood. Ella's horrific childhood was just beginning.

The one-bedroom house didn't have enough space for two adults and two children. Dad and his brother Richard built a single-story, three-bedroom home. However, moving to a bigger house still wasn't enough for Ella to escape our dad's abuse.

Once, Dad was taking his weekly Sunday afternoon nap. Anna and Ella were playing in the basement. Like all little toddler girls do, they started playing loudly. They accidentally woke up the badger. In a furious rage, he grabbed Ella and began beating her head against the concrete wall. She screamed in terror. The more she cried, the harder he slammed her into the wall.

While living here, my parents had four more children: Jerry, Peggy, Trudy, and Jolene. This is where Mom got their first little Chihuahua puppy, Bimbo. The adorable puppy was initially excited to have his own family to love. Within hours, Bimbo realized that an evil badger lived among them. This badger was teaching his children how to be mean to others and to animals.

Bimbo was a small indoor doggie. Whenever my dad was around, Bimbo tried to hide. Dad became jealous that my mom gave love to Bimbo. He immediately became cruel to the little poochie. But then again, who wasn't he cruel to? He wanted all the attention. No pooch was going to take that from him.

Whenever Bimbo got close, Dad kicked him — not a gentle kick either, but enough to send Bimbo flying across the room. There hasn't been an official diagnosis for my sister Ella's broken ribs. However, Mom told me that Bimbo had broken ribs and broken legs because of Dad kicking and throwing him all the time.

With my parents now having six children, they moved to a 5-acre farm. This two-story house was larger, but had a long driveway that was hard to keep clear of snow. They didn't have tractors or farm equipment for snow removal.

Being stranded for weeks, they couldn't go into town. Dad couldn't get to work. They needed to get groceries to feed all these kids. Besides, Mom had just given birth to her seventh baby and was already pregnant with her eighth. Susan and Harlan were both born in the same year, with Susan arriving in January and Harlan in December.

The winters were long. Everyone felt cooped up inside. Bimbo received massive amounts of abuse and suffered internal injuries. He could barely walk, eat, drink, or go to the bathroom. Bimbo accidentally went potty in the house. Dad was the first up in the mornings and discovered Bimbo's mess. In a fit of rage, he grabbed Bimbo and shoved his nose into the poop. Then, of course, as all people with rage do, he beat Bimbo and threw him across the room.

Bimbo slept behind the wood-burning stove to stay safe from the badger and to keep warm. One morning, Mom found Bimbo had died during the night. Tears welled up in her eyes, and her grief was beyond belief. She realized that the man she called her husband had slowly murdered their little poochie. She loved Bimbo dearly and ultimately couldn't protect her poochie from the jealous monster we called our dad.

Mom became more rigid, demanding, distant, and unavailable. She tried to control what she could in her extremely out-of-control marriage to a rage-filled man. She was afraid to stand up for herself, her children, or Bimbo. Living with a man full of jealousy and rage caused Mom to go into a mental paralysis whenever he was around.

~ Cinder-Ella ~

Bimbo died from severe physical abuse, broken bones, and internal bleeding. I'm sure that my sister Ella many times wished she could die too. The cruelty that Dad inflicted on baby Ella never ended. His extreme abuse of her never stopped throughout her childhood and teenage years. He beat her down with his angry, vulgar words.

Not long after Bimbo died, my parents moved to a 5-acre chicken farm. It had a shorter driveway. It was also a two-story, four-bedroom house with three bedrooms upstairs, one on the main floor, and a basement. This house was my childhood home. This is where my mom had her last seven children — Ben, me, Danielle, Jesse, Pete, Alex, and Sadie.

Early in their marriage, Mom lost her glitter eyes for my dad. Day by day, she grew more emotionally, physically, and romantically repulsed by him. By the time she became pregnant with Ella, she had begun rejecting Dad's romantic advances. She used any excuse she could think of to avoid being intimate with him. She said she was pregnant or too tired.

He became furious and frustrated as he continued to get rejected. Baby Ella didn't stand a chance. His hatred of her started before she was born, and it never went away. He called her horrible names, taunted her, hit her, and sexually abused her. He stole every ounce of decency and privacy from her as he beat her into an empty shell.

Dad also taught my oldest brother, Jerry, to abuse Ella. They teased her, chanting mean, rhyming names. Many times, they called her "Smella Ella." Thinking it was hilarious, they hollered, "Opie," since it rhymed with "Dopey." They were saying she was a bimbo. Ella spent a lot of time crying. Her eyes were always red and swollen. Dad and Jerry gave her the nickname "Pig Eyes."

Because of the abuse she endured, Ella likely suffered early brain damage. She struggled to follow directions and often forgot to do her chores. Mom and Anna thought Ella was lazy. Slamming a child's head against the wall can cause head trauma. Shaken baby syndrome can cause a range of brain malfunctions. They couldn't see her head trauma, deep depression, or heartache caused by Dad and Jerry's ongoing abuse. They didn't understand why they had to keep telling her what to do and how to do it. Why on earth was she so slow at completing her jobs?

Ella couldn't focus and struggled to concentrate on the overwhelming number of chores assigned to her. Mom and Anna became abusive toward Ella in their effort to make her work faster. They yelled at her and sometimes called her names.

Ella had no one to protect her. Everyone around her seemed to hate her. Mom gave her many extra chores as punishment for her laziness. They scolded her if she didn't meet their standards. They made her redo it until she got it right. Ella was walking on eggshells, never knowing who might hurt her next. She tried to do everything correctly, but they also wanted it done fast. Her head was spinning with fear and confusion. Ella became the family's *Cinder-Ella.*

One day, Mom came home from the hospital with another baby. Ella stopped working and went to peek at the newest addition. Mom snapped, "What are you looking at? Get back to work!" Ella was to have nothing to do with the babies. She was the worker. She was *Cinder-Ella* — a lazy, good-for-nothing, burdensome, worthless child, who did nothing right or fast enough.

If Ella didn't do a chore correctly, she couldn't eat until she did it right. Jerry stole food off her plate before she got there. Even when she could join right away, Jerry still stole her food.

Ella was often hungry. She didn't think Mom would miss one of those plump, tasty-looking peaches on the counter. She took one and hid it under her shirt to sneak away and fill her tummy a bit. Mom was an efficient food planner. She definitely noticed that her peach was missing, as she had planned to make peach pies. She had purchased exactly the amount that she needed. When Mom saw that one peach was gone, she lost her temper. Somehow, she knew Ella had taken it. Mom harshly scolded her, and Ella never heard the end of it.

My parents were poor. No one could take food between meals without asking. Mom had plans for every food item. Now she had to make either one pie — or two pies with a small amount of peaches. From then on, none of us dared take food without asking. We all knew money was tight. We all saw how our mom seemingly scraped food off the floor to feed our enormous family.

Jerry was under our dad's wing. Like father, like son, Jerry became abusive toward all the girls. He picked on us, stole food from us, and scared us half to death. Jerry took Harlan and Ben under his wing and trained them in his same ways. Jerry always flicked our ears from behind. His attitude said, "I'm the oldest, and you are a little twerp." He also swiped food from my plate. We were all starving by the time we sat down to eat, and having our bully brother steal our food was upsetting.

I was a screamer. Whenever anyone was cruel, I screamed at the top of my lungs. It was a shrill and long scream. The pitch was so high that some of them had to cover their ears. Sometimes, after someone hurt me, I didn't eat fast because my heart was hurting. Jerry took my slow eating as a sign that I wasn't hungry. Snatching the food off my plate, he said, "I'll eat that if you aren't going to." I learned not to need much food. However, I knew if I were to survive, I couldn't sit near Jerry.

One day, when I was 7 or 8, the ol' family station wagon broke down. Mom had to borrow Jerry's car to go to the grocery store. I went with her, and I stayed in the car while she ran into the store. I opened the glove compartment while I was waiting, and I felt appalled at what I found inside. There were pornographic pictures inside that shocked me deep in my soul. When Mom came back out of the store, I gave her the pictures. I am still scarred by what I saw. Jerry started calling me a "little weasel." He made it clear he thought I was an annoying little tattletale.

Jerry was always looking for new ways to play pranks on Ella. It was her job to gather all the eggs and wash the dirty ones. Jerry often took Harlan and Ben up on top of the garage with a five-gallon bucket of water. They hid on one side of the roof and peeked over the crest. Ella couldn't see them. As she was returning from her chores, they dumped the water on her. They laughed about how they got her good. Ella came into the house drenched in water. Changing her clothes had to wait, as Mom and Anna needed help to prepare supper.

They waited a few weeks, then they'd drench Ella again when she wasn't expecting it. Whenever I saw those boys sneaking around with a bucket of water or climbing on top of the garage, I warned Ella. However, I couldn't let them know I was telling on them. They'd have treated me even worse.

Once, I found some empty egg flats to use as an excuse to warn Ella. Nobody went to the henhouse without a reason. If I went empty-handed, they'd realize I was warning her. I pretended I didn't see them and acted as if I were just following orders. I kept my distance from them to avoid getting water dumped on me. Handing the flats to Ella, I warned her and hurried back to the house. On my way back, I pretended to be surprised to see them. I fooled them. They didn't catch on that I had just warned Ella.

Another time, I snuck around the back of the chicken house. This route wasn't my first choice because I had to go past a massive pile of chicken manure. I tried to warn Ella whenever I could. I felt it was my duty to help protect her. They were all so mean to her.

Sunday mornings were prime time when they picked on Ella. Dad and Jerry were both home because we couldn't work on Sundays. The only work allowed was cooking food and feeding the farm animals. They attacked Ella as she was washing dishes after breakfast. It was her daily chore to clean all the dishes after every meal. She had her back to the room. My dad or Jerry would sneak up behind her, reach both hands up her skirt, and rip her underwear down to the floor.

It was the church's rule that the girls had to wear skirts. This made it easy for them to abuse Ella. Sometimes, she was on her period. Ella cried every time they degraded her. She was so embarrassed. They stripped her of her dignity in front of the whole family.

Mom often yelled at the older girls for using too many menstrual pads because they were expensive. Ella, to avoid scolding, started using an empty plastic bread bag under the pad to reduce changes. The bag caught the blood that overflowed and helped keep her clothes from getting soiled. She was trying to do whatever it took to use fewer pads and avoid getting scolded. Her period was heavy because of extreme stress. She couldn't rest for a day or two. Mom expected her to, every day, no matter what, continue to be *Cinder-Ella.*

Dad and the boys started calling her "Sack Packer" after they saw she used a bag. Seeing this bag gave them reason to tear her underwear down more often. They claimed they needed to check if she had a sack in there. As Ella got older, our dad became even more sexually abusive toward her.

One dreadful Sunday morning, Dad stormed out of the bathroom. Holding a used pad in his hand, he stomped over to Ella as she was washing the dishes. He yelled at her, "Whose is this? Is it yours? It's not full!" He showed everyone the bloody pad. Then he shoved it right up near Ella's face. He taunted her and demanded to know if she was on her period. He kept snarling at her angrily, asking her over and over if it was hers. Poor Ella was so embarrassed that she started to cry.

Dad threw the pad down. He attacked her violently. He pulled her to the floor and tore her underwear off. The whole time, he yelled, saying she was a "dirty heifer that needed to be cleaned." He reached for the dish soap, took one of her ankles, and jerked her half upside down. He squirted the soap onto her, grabbed the scrub brush, and violently scrubbed her private area.

I screamed repeatedly for him to stop. It seemed like everyone around me was laughing. Those few minutes felt like they lasted forever. They are indeed minutes that have become forever burned into my memory. Ella was constantly being abused, traumatized, and violated. She received no love as a baby, child, or teenager. How did she ever survive such horrific abuse? I pray that the day comes quickly when she will find eternal peace in heaven.

I can't imagine what other abuse Ella suffered in that chicken house from Dad and Jerry behind closed doors. It's better not to know, lest my heart be ripped out from my very chest.

I had to detach to recount the things regarding Ella. I wrote as an outsider looking in. I was actually an insider and a witness who saw and heard all of her vicious abuse. I felt, and still feel, all of her fear and pain.

~ Ducks in a Row ~

We had a vicious monster in our home. None of us could stop him from attacking. We were just kids. The trauma we endured is more than most people can understand unless they've lived through what we experienced every day.

Mom couldn't stop Dad. Many times, she stood by helplessly. Whenever she tried to intervene, his rage intensified even further. Things spiraled out of control. Sometimes she got hurt, or one of us kids got our head slammed against the wall. Other times, we got hit by something thrown at us.

As a child, Mom didn't have many toys, except for a special doll she received when she was seven years old, and a new bike when she was twelve. She rarely played, as she mainly went to school, church, did her homework, and worked hard at home on the farm.

Fear of hell, fire, and damnation became deeply rooted in my mom's heart. Every Sunday, the preacher told her she was a worthless sinner and unworthy of God's love. They taught her to pray to God for forgiveness of her many sins and to save her soul from hell.

Mom gave birth to a new baby every year. Her church said birth control is a sin, and we should do nothing to prevent children. They said God commanded her to be fruitful, multiply, and replenish the earth. She thought it was pleasing to God to keep having children. According to the church, she had no choice.

She believed God predestined every child born to her, so she should not complain. Her church told her to be thankful God had blessed her with children. My mom was the "Old woman who lived in a shoe. She had so many children, she didn't know what to do."

They said divorce was a sin. She became trapped until death do they part. If Mom could have divorced, none of this terrible abuse would have happened. However, even if her church had allowed divorce, she couldn't have supported everyone by herself.

Mom wasn't able to give us the love, comfort, protection, and compassion we desperately needed. We received no nurturing. She had no time to comfort us when we got hurt. After a sibling was cruel, she yelled, "Knock it off." However, she didn't give the child a proper punishment. She made no one apologize. Sometimes, they had to write sentences about God's displeasure with their behavior. Mom wrote the first sentence at the top of the paper, and the child, usually one of the boys, had to copy her sentence 50 times as their punishment.

Nobody ever said "please" and "thank you." Our parents didn't teach us how to embrace or express our feelings. They didn't show us how to work through problems. Everything got swept under the rug, which kept everyone simmering inside, holding grudges, and talking behind each other's backs.

Nobody ever said, "I love you." We weren't supposed to love ourselves. If we looked at ourselves in the mirror, Mom scolded us for being proud. We were to use the mirror only for necessities. Her church taught that loving oneself was prideful, and pride was a sin. This harmful teaching was part of the reason we didn't receive the gentle, patient, compassionate, understanding, and forgiving love that all children need to thrive.

Mom loved each of us, like all mothers love their children. Still, with the heavy workload and the horrifying abuse happening in our home, she could only survive and provide us with basic needs like food, clothing, and shelter.

Mom had no one to protect her, and she couldn't defend us. We heard from our dad that we were worthless children who deserved death. Our church said that we are worthless sinners unworthy of God's love. They said God is an angry, stern, judgmental God who sends most people to hell to burn forever. Nobody ever made us feel special.

My mom was strict about praying at mealtime, upon waking, and before bed. Sometimes I'd hear her praying before she fell asleep, begging God to please save our souls from hell. The sad irony of her prayers is that our home was already a living hell.

Her church taught her that God predestined everyone, even before they were born, to go either to heaven or hell. Her pleading with God, trying to change His mind, showed me she loved us. She didn't want any of us to burn in hellfire forever.

Mom was barely holding on emotionally. Still, she did a fantastic job of taking care of everyone. She always worked hard and made sure we had a roof over our heads, clothes to wear, and food to eat. On Saturdays, she often had us girls help her bake cookies, cakes, and other treats so she could have snacks ready for us when we got home from school.

We had 17 people in our family. Anna was a second mother to the younger children. My mom always ran around the house — working, organizing, delegating, cooking, baking, doing laundry, grocery shopping, managing finances, and gardening. She also made sure that everyone completed their outside chores. She had an enormous task of keeping all her *ducks in a row.*

She was an unstoppable, incredible workhorse and the hardest worker I've ever known. She was an excellent organizer. Knowing everything that needed to be done, she either handled it herself or made it happen. I don't know how she had time to take a shower. Her focus was on organizing how everything was to be accomplished.

She was mentally sharp. Her brain and body continued to operate at full speed. How anyone could carry such a massive life load is beyond my imagination. We kids were her workers. There's no way she could have managed it all without us. Then again, without us, she wouldn't have had to!

Mom had two miscarriages. I'm sure that they resulted from massive stress, or our dad having a physical altercation with her. He didn't want to keep having all these kids. Many times, I remember him holding a butcher knife and threatening to run it through her pregnant belly to kill her and the baby inside of her.

Mom's plate became full. She grew overworked and sleep-deprived. She never complained. When her plate filled up, she swapped it for a larger platter. When her platter became overloaded, she replaced it with a serving tray.

Mom often yelled to get everyone to cooperate. She had no extra time for disobedient kids who were talking back or trying to avoid their work. She had no patience for laziness.

Mom maintained a strict routine. She ran a tight ship and kept all her *ducks in a row.* She was trudging through life, emotionally detached, and running her ship in a provide-and-survive mode only.

I often wished Mom didn't have to work so hard. I daydreamed about buying her a nice house when I grew up. Her house slippers always looked worn out. At mealtime, she made sure we had enough food. Then, she served herself last.

After Dad had one of his blowups, I'd find Mom sitting alone, either on her bed or on the organ bench. She was crying and looked so sad. I tried to comfort her by asking what was wrong. She couldn't explain; it would have taken years to do so. Everything was wrong! I knew that, so I sat close beside her and told her it would be okay. Crying with her, I felt so sad to see my mom hurting so badly. I hurt for her and wished things could be different. I loved her.

She felt comforted. As she wiped her tears and blew her nose, she said, "There's no use crying over spilled milk. All the work that needs doing won't finish itself, so I'd best get after it." If I could have carried her burden, I would have. I helped around the house and on the farm. I tried to stay strong and lighten her load. The weight of the world lay heavy on her shoulders.

We planted three enormous gardens every spring and summer. We prepared the gardens using the tiller and created rows with the hoe. After planting, we watered and weeded twice a week. Once we harvested the vegetables, we cleaned and stored them. Half of them were placed in quart jars, and we sealed them in the pressure canner. Then we put them on the basement shelves. Some vegetables had to be put into containers and stored in the large basement freezer.

We filled large gunny sacks with potatoes and onions and kept them in the chicken house cooler. Our summers were so full of work that we didn't know what summer vacation from school meant. How was all this work a vacation?

We had many apple trees on our farm. There were several Saturdays when we picked apples. As we collected the ones on the ground, we checked them for worms. We threw those over the fence into the cornfield.

The apples had to be washed and cut into quarters. Then we boiled them in a large pot until they were soft. After that, we scooped them into the manual applesauce strainer. The wooden roller squeezed all the applesauce through the sieve into the large bowl below. What remained in the strainer were peels and seeds. Finally, we poured the applesauce into canning jars and placed them in the pressure canner to be stored in the basement.

Mom managed the enormous tasks of shopping, meal planning, and preparing breakfast, lunch, and dinner. There were many hungry mouths. I bet the question she heard most was, "What's for dinner?"

Just feeding everyone was a full-time job. Mom needed all the help she could get. The girls had to help with the cooking and setting the table. Amazingly, we had every meal ready at the same time each day. My mom was pretty strict about, "If you don't work, you don't eat!"

Cleaning up after meals took 45 minutes. There were many dishes, pots, and pans to wash and dry. We also had to sweep the floor after each meal. No food ever got thrown away; we ate every crumb. On rare occasions when there were leftovers, we stored them in the refrigerator for the next meal.

All scraps and bones went to the dogs and cats outside. We threw all vegetable peelings and fat to the hogs. Since we had mashed potatoes almost every night, we girls became expert potato peelers. We needed 10 to 15 pounds of potatoes peeled, washed, cut, boiled, and mashed to feed our entire family.

The laundry we had to do on Saturdays was overwhelming. It seemed like we could never finish. We had an enclosed porch area off the kitchen that also served as the laundry room. We had two huge 75-gallon barrels where everyone tossed their dirty clothes throughout the week. These barrels had no bottoms.

We washed ten huge loads of clothes in the washing machine. To conserve electricity, we could use the dryer only during the winter months. We took all the clothes outside and hung them on the clothesline. Once they were dry, we retrieved them and brought them back inside to fold, hang, and put away. Laundry itself was an all-day job. Between washing, hanging, and folding clothes, we still had to complete all the other chores for our busy workday.

Mom washed everyone's hair on Saturdays. She used the kitchen sink with the kids lying on the counter. I was always intrigued by the hair under her armpits. Everyone took a bath at night to get ready for church. There was a showerhead in the porch for the older kids. Since there wasn't a bathtub, Mom used a large, circular metal washtub in the shower area to bathe the younger kids.

To conserve water, we all shared the same bathwater. However, Mom boiled a pot of water on the stove to make the bath warm again for each new round of kids. It was best to get the first bath. By the time the third batch got in, the water was filthy. We can't say the third group of kids got a proper bath — a mud bath, maybe!

When I was about 9 or 10 years old, my parents added a larger bathroom. It had a toilet, bathtub, sink, and storage shelves. The new bathroom offered privacy with a locking door. Finally, nobody entered while we were using it.

~ Full Nest ~

On our chicken farm, we had a huge chicken house with 2,000 egg-laying chickens. They were in suspended cages that hung from the rafters. We pushed a cart down the aisles to gather the eggs. There was a big red barn, a silo, and a big hog house. We had a few other buildings and sheds, which were used for storing machinery, tools, or animals.

Dad had a variety of animals. He had two cows that my parents milked twice a day. They got rid of them after they kept getting teat infections. They bought milk from a nearby dairy farmer instead. We had sheep at one point. Dad never sheared them properly, and they ended up with many cuts all over their bodies. They looked like sheep from a horror movie when he finished shaving them. He either sold the wool or used it for warmth for the baby pigs, calves, and goats.

I remember having pigs for a couple of years. We also had destructive billy goats, rabbits, cats, dogs, and many other random animals that he impulsively bought when he went to the sale barn.

Dad tried to be a farmer. He should have focused on one type of animal instead of many. Of all the animals, the worst was the big, scary bull. Dad was probably trying to raise calves to sell. I was very relieved when he took that bull to auction.

Near our farmhouse, a detached two-car garage housed our dogs and cats. It was also where we parked our vehicle. My parents had a long station wagon with three full bench seats. We entered the first and second-row seats through the side doors. The third row faced backwards, and we climbed in through the back door. Fitting fifteen children into the wagon for church was quite a challenge. We were all squished in. The youngest kids had to sit on laps. Everyone argued the entire way to and from church, exchanging snide comments. Nobody enjoyed sitting so close together.

Between the garage and the chicken house, there was an outdoor potty shack. We didn't use it often because it smelled terrible, and there were always swarms of flies in there. Jerry eventually removed the toilet, filled the hole with dirt, and placed a makeshift board on top to serve as a floor. We used the shack as a playhouse. I took the younger kids outside to play as much as possible to keep them out of harm's way. We played house in the silo or the barn attic. It was fun pretending to be parents and kids. We pretended to bake, cook, and eat dinner. We also played school and church together.

Sometimes we played church on the steps. We took turns being the preacher. I wish I could remember what we said as we stood there acting all religious and preaching our little sermon to the misbehaving kids who were sitting on the stairs.

The winters up north brought mountains of snow and blizzards. Since our house lacked good insulation, the weather inside and outside was almost the same. Being indoors at least kept us out of the wind. Our home had a furnace in the basement that blew warm air up to the main living area through register vents. Many of us kids sat on the kitchen floor, wrapped in blankets, on top of the registers, trying to stay warm. The furnace heat didn't reach the upstairs bedrooms. To heat upstairs, warm air rose through the ceiling registers. It also helped to leave the stairway door open.

My parents were poor, so we had to conserve gas, electricity, and water. The main floor of the house wasn't warm, so little heat rose upwards. Mom gave us blankets and quilts, but they were cold when we got into bed. We felt frozen, and it took lots of shivering to fall asleep.

Many of us wet the bed. Everyone received a small padded quilt to use as their pee blanket. Each morning, we hung the blanket over the staircase banister to dry. Often, it wasn't dry by bedtime. We either had to sleep on a partially damp blanket or put it in the dryer. During the day, going up and down the stairs involved dodging to avoid getting dripped on from the soaking-wet pee blankets hanging on the railing.

My parents had nine girls and six boys. There was one large bedroom and two small bedrooms upstairs. Anna had her own room, and I slept with her. The large room had four beds, and all the other girls crowded into it. Jerry had the other small room. Harlan and Ben moved in there after Jerry left home. When Anna married, I moved into the big room. The next oldest girl got the small bedroom. As each child moved out, the new oldest child would move into the vacated bedroom.

After Anna left, Trudy took care of all the babies. Jesse, Pete, Alex, and Sadie were the four youngest kids. When Mom started working overnight shifts at the nursing home, Trudy babysat in the living room downstairs. All four had colic. Trudy spent many sleepless nights calming them with walking, rocking, bouncing, and feeding. When one kid fell asleep, another woke up. To make things harder, Dad always yelled at her to keep the kids quiet. Trudy became resentful about caring for babies that weren't hers. She wasn't supposed to be a teenage mom to someone else's babies.

Although forced into this mother position, Trudy did an excellent job taking care of the fussy babies. She lost a lot of sleep and still had to go to school the next day. As Trudy grew more worn out, she became withdrawn. She started giving Mom the silent treatment and wouldn't speak a word for weeks. This made the atmosphere even more uncomfortable. Everyone was walking on eggshells.

Trudy, in her silent rebellion, refused to answer when spoken to. If she needed to talk to Mom, she addressed her by her first name. Trudy felt angry. She had lost respect for Mom. All of us girls helped with the babies during the day. We had to help with feeding and diaper changes. We used cloth diapers and had to rinse them in the toilet before putting them in the washer.

Our farmhouse took a real beating. It became more run-down each year. All the boys were rowdy and destructive. You'd think they were born in a barn. I often heard Mom get frustrated as everything kept breaking. She yelled, "What next?" The boys had BB guns. They shot out the windows of the outside buildings. Twice, they shot a house window as well. Things broke faster than we could fix them.

Feeling overwhelmed and upset, Mom would yell, "Oh, for crying out loud!" She wanted to cry, but she had to stay strong and hold this madhouse together. Everything was falling apart. She pushed her tears away. She shoved them deep down inside herself. Provide and survive — provide and survive.

If she fell apart, the roof would cave in on our *nest*. Her only choice was to turn her overwhelming desire to cry into anger and frustration. She hollered, "Get out of the kitchen!" The boys were always underfoot, fighting and bullying each other. Mom was on the brink of losing it. She often said, "Whew! I feel like I'm losing my mind!" She got no breaks. Her head was spinning from the weight of the heavy load she carried.

~ Rotten Egg ~

I have to give Dad credit for going to his job at the cardboard factory every day. He provided money for everyone to eat and have shelter. He worked hard and never missed a day of work. On many Saturdays, he worked half-days. Nobody looked forward to his return home. Everyone's hair rose on the backs of our necks as he drove up the driveway. We never knew if he had been drinking alcohol, so we watched him as he stepped out of his truck. We wanted to see whether he would be drunkenly abusive or just his regular abusive.

When Dad came home, he did some farm chores. As he found things broken, he became furious. Money was tight. Now he had to fix more things. His plate was full. He wanted these destructive kids out of his way.

Dad's vulgar vocabulary was his most noticeable trait, and we should have been born cussing like sailors. His favorites were: "Get the hell out of my way!" and "You GDSOB!" We were on edge with fear, knowing his explosive anger could strike unexpectedly. His anger showed in everything he said and did. He was the most unpleasant man I've known.

If we got in his way, he threatened us with harm or death. He had many shotguns and intimidated us with them. We grew up with a killer. If Dad had carried a pistol in a holster on his hip, nobody would be alive. The pitchfork was one of his favorite weapons. He often threatened to run us through with it. Everyone hated him, and some kids taunted and egged him on.

Dad had a triple personality. He appeared psychopathic or at least had serious mental issues. He was a *rotten egg.* During most of his episodes, he would grab the nearest object and chase us. If we ran fast enough, we didn't get hit. However, he threw his weapon. Usually, he missed because we had become expert runners. We learned to weave from side to side to avoid his crowbar or hammer. We all came in first place during school races.

One Saturday, I hoped to get Dad and the boys to help me fix my bike. I must have said something wrong. He started cursing at me. He picked up the crowbar. Terrified, I ran as fast as I could. As I was running, the crowbar whizzed inches from my head. I was in extreme danger. I kept running until I reached the edge of the farm. My heart pounded in my chest. For hours, I hid in the trees at the farm's edge. Finally, I crept back toward the house to see if it was safe to return.

Once, Mom got a little wiener dog. She was protective of it. I could tell she loved that poochie a lot. Looking back, I'm sure that after Bimbo's death, she wouldn't allow anyone to be mean to her new puppy. One day, we were digging in the dirt with sticks and playing with the wiener dog. Out of the blue, the dog bit me. Shocked, I hit it with my stick, and it yelped in pain. The other kids ran to tell Mom. I ran into the cornfield to hide. If she found out, I'd be in big trouble. I stayed in that spooky cornfield for hours. Finally, I crept to the edge and lay there watching the house. I didn't dare go up there.

They hollered at me for supper a few times, but I was too scared of Mom. When they yelled again, they hollered I wasn't in trouble and could come back. They said she wasn't mad. I didn't get into trouble. However, I stayed away from that dog.

Whenever Mom went to the grocery store, she tried to get back as quickly as possible. She always felt anxiety about being gone. She never knew what terrible things might happen. Sometimes, Dad attacked all of us at once. He used our big kitchen table as his weapon. He used it to corral and smash us. Eventually, we learned to fight back as a team. We all pushed the table away from us toward him so we could escape and run outside. We ran into the wooded area and hid behind the trees.

We were worried Dad might kill us while we were asleep. Every night, we went to bed terrified. Some nights, we balanced a large metal clothes barrel lid on top of our bedroom door. If he opened it, the lid would fall and make a loud banging noise. Waking up wouldn't have helped if he had a shotgun. However, it gave us enough peace of mind to fall asleep.

One Saturday, when I was eight, we were all eating lunch. Dad was in one of his horrible moods. He may have been drinking beer. A fight broke out. Dad became so angry that he threatened to kill us. Right here and right now. As he stood up angrily from the table, he snarled that he was getting the gun to shoot us all dead. He stormed out of the kitchen, through the enclosed porch area, and toward the basement stairs where the shotguns were hanging. We all knew he would do it. There was no doubt about it.

Jerry, now 18, rushed after Dad to stop him. We all ran after them to see if we could help. Dad had already taken the shotgun down from the rack. Jerry was on the stairs, trying to pry it away from him. As Jerry pulled the gun from him, the force was so strong that Dad fell down the basement stairs.

Jerry stood up to Dad that day. We were thankful Jerry did that. He saved our lives. If Jerry hadn't saved us, Dad would have killed us all. After Jerry helped him up the stairs and made sure he didn't grab another gun, Dad went out to the chicken house to lick his wounds. He calmed down for a day or two. However, it wasn't long before he returned to his old self. After Anna and Jerry moved out, we lost our protectors and had to fend for ourselves.

There were many violent incidents, especially during mealtime. Dad flew off the handle at the slightest provocation. When he did, it was best to duck under the table. He grabbed anything within reach. Back then, we bought everything in glass jars. He threw applesauce, ketchup, and pickle jars. Glass shattered, and the contents splattered everywhere. The mess after these episodes was enormous. Splatter was all over the kitchen — on the cupboards, countertops, floor, and ceiling. Nobody cleaned the ceiling. The splatters stayed up there, and more condiments just got added with each of his furious outbursts.

Mom was strict about reading the Bible after every meal. Sometimes, in her hope of converting Dad, she mentioned how he was supposed to be the family's religious leader. Dad occasionally demanded that she give him the Bible. It never ended well. He tried to read it respectfully, but it was so out of character that the kids started laughing at him. Sometimes he shed a few tears. The boys snickered at him. Dad exploded. As he stood up in his rage, his chair flew backward. He shoved the table forward and threw the Bible at the kid who was taunting him. The Bible became ripped and torn from all the times he threw it.

Dad married my mom without realizing all the strict rules her church would require of him. Mom likely made a stipulation before they married that he attend church with her. She strictly followed her church's doctrine and rules. It was all she knew. Dad didn't grow up with these strict church rules and wouldn't follow them. He sneaked behind Mom's back and listened to the radio. He drank alcohol, looked at pornography, and smoked tobacco. The no birth-control rule likely caught him by surprise. I doubt he saw himself having so many children. From one *rotten egg,* 15 *scrambled eggs* were born.

Mom was stern about our listening only to church music. Dad rebelled against her rules. He had learned the accordion as a kid. Sometimes, he would take it out and play it. The songs he played weren't from Mom's church songbook. It wasn't long before she yelled at him to put his accordion away. She called his music worldly and didn't want him playing it in our house. She felt hostile toward his playing. We enjoyed listening to the few songs he could play. We kept asking him to play another song, but Mom won with her yelling.

When Mom ran errands, some kids turned the radio to a different station. They watched for her return so they could turn it off to avoid getting caught. Sometimes, they forgot to turn the dial back to her church station. The next time she turned it on, they got caught. No one admitted to doing it, and some of them blamed it on our dad.

Mom became skilled at playing the organ when she was younger. When we grew older, the church asked her to play at church two Sunday evenings each month. Now, adding more to her already overflowing plate, she had to find time to practice the songs.

Although she enjoyed playing and it brought her happiness, performing in front of the congregation was a stressful experience. She couldn't make a mistake. The people at her church expected perfection when singing their holy songs. If she messed up a song, she would be the topic of gossip during every coffee break for months. If she made too many mistakes, the church members would vote her out. When they built the church, they designed it so that the organist wouldn't be visible from the sanctuary. Only the minister, elders, and deacons could parade themselves before the people.

~ Cock-a-too-da-loo ~

Dad didn't realize that his cruelty would destroy intimacy. Mom being constantly pregnant and crying babies flooding in also caused romance to dwindle. She didn't want to keep having more babies as her church demanded. She likely avoided intimacy to prevent having more children. All she wanted was to sleep before the babies woke up crying.

If she ever loved him, Mom could never have kept loving such a horrible man. Daily, the hatred between them grew stronger. The fighting became more horrifying each day. Mom pitted us against Dad, and Dad did the same to Mom.

Our old farmhouse had heat register holes in the floors of the upstairs bedrooms. These allowed heat to rise from below into the upper rooms. Having these holes meant we could hear everything happening downstairs. When I was 11 years old, Danielle, Jolene, and I slept above my parents' room. Many nights, we heard them fighting. We listened as Dad got angry, first raising his voice, then yelling, followed by a string of curse words. If we had been sleeping, their arguing woke us up. Sometimes, we tiptoed over to the hole to listen more closely and see if Mom was safe. We knew and avoided every spot on the floor that would creak.

It was terrifying to hear Dad so angry. I worried Mom would get hurt or killed. I was little and couldn't help her. The fighting shocked my sisters and me, and we covered the register hole with books and blankets to muffle the sound of their arguing. Sometimes I put my heavy blanket over my ears so I wouldn't hear them.

Dad was trying to be intimate. When Mom said no, he got angry. It usually ended with his throwing pots and pans. We heard glass breaking. Many times, Mom likely gave in out of fear. However, when she didn't, Dad destroyed the kitchen. The sexual fighting we all endured is something children don't walk away from unscathed.

My dad wouldn't accept that after having a baby, she needs to heal. He was a perverted man who believed he could have intimacy whenever he wanted. Being turned down made him furious. Sometimes, he tried to be sickeningly sweet to her so she would give in to him at night. Eventually, she stopped falling for it, and the fights increased.

Every night, I had a nightmare about a large bull chasing me down the chicken house aisles. When I woke up, my heart was pounding. I went downstairs. It was extremely cold upstairs, and I couldn't get back to sleep after waking up frightened by the bull. Mom turned the heat way down at night to save on propane costs. During those bitterly cold winters, it felt like I would freeze to death. I grabbed my pillow and blanket and made my new bed downstairs on the hard kitchen floor, on top of the warm register.

Dad was sleeping by then, so I felt reasonably safe. I slowly turned the heat dial until I heard the furnace ignite. Now, I could warm up enough to fall asleep. Sometimes, Mom woke up from hearing the furnace kick on. She came out and dialed it back down. When I first started coming downstairs in the middle of the night, she hollered at me to get back upstairs. I listened, but I couldn't get warm or fall asleep. After about 30 minutes, I went back down again.

I faked being asleep when Mom came out to adjust the dial. It worked. She thought I was sleeping and didn't hear her. She left me and went back to bed. Being downstairs also helped me stay closer to her and keep her safe. Dad hated it when I started sleeping downstairs. If he got up to use the bathroom, or in the mornings when he woke up, he deliberately kicked me as he walked past. My new bed was now 15 feet from their bedroom. It was located right under the telephone in case I needed to call the police.

After Mom started working nights, I just went to bed in my little corner. It became my bed. I was warmer, and no longer had nightmares. Sleeping on the hard kitchen floor even helped me stop wetting the bed. When I woke up shivering, the bathroom was only 20 feet away. I could then return to the warm register.

After many years of abuse, Mom avoided sleeping in the same bed as Dad. The fighting decreased when she started working nights. I'm sure they needed more income, but I believe she did it to escape his advances.

Dad hated it when Mom started working. He accused her of cheating on him. During her first month, he jumped into his truck and chased her down the road. He almost ran her off the road. He followed her to make sure she wasn't meeting a boyfriend. Mom slept at the nursing home between her rounds, and also at home in the mornings. When she didn't have to work, she slept on the couch.

My dad used my mom's night shifts as his chance to drink beer. He had already been giving us cigarettes out in the chicken house, and he had also been giving the boys beer. But now, with Mom working the 10 pm shift, he started giving us beer after she left.

One night, I passed out from alcohol. When I fainted, I fell and hit my head on the concrete cistern cover outside our back door. When I woke up, my sundress had slipped down, leaving me exposed in front of my abusive dad. It was a moment of shame I never want to repeat. I felt embarrassed and quickly went to bed. I never drank with him again. It was never that fun anyway. He was never nice to be around.

To save money, Mom bought day-old bread. When Dad was with us, he flirted with and talked in a syrupy sweet manner to the lady at the checkout counter. He always threatened our mom that he was going to visit the bread store lady. Whenever he was late coming home from work, Mom asked him if he had stopped by to see his girlfriend.

After several years of working nights, Mom started working days. She drove the morning and afternoon bus routes for the church's private school. Instead of sleeping in her bedroom, she continued sleeping on the couch. She avoided sleeping with the person she had grown to hate.

This infuriated Dad beyond belief. I will never forget the day I stayed home from school because I was sick. My mom wasn't home yet from driving her bus route. I was resting in the recliner when I heard him banging drawers and throwing things in the kitchen. He was yelling, cursing, and slamming things around. His anger grew by the minute, and I was ready to face his wrath. I immediately went into survival mode. I closed my eyes and pretended to be sleeping.

As I peeped through my eyelids, I saw him storm into the living room with a huge butcher knife held up in the air. My heart almost jumped out of my chest. Instead of coming at me, he went to the couch and stabbed the knife into the cushions repeatedly. He was cussing and yelling at my mom, who wasn't there. As he screamed insane words, he stabbed her over and over. He hated her so much for not sleeping with him. Now, he wasn't only threatening to kill her; he had done it in his mind. I knew he had entered a new level of rage. This was something I hadn't seen before.

It was no longer angry threats, but he was now premeditating how to do it. The words that I heard as he was stabbing his knife gave me the chills to the bone. I had witnessed a murder — the murder of my mom. When Mom returned home, I told her what I had seen and heard. I showed her all the cuts in the couch where he had stabbed her. I warned her that he was planning to kill her. Dad was different after this incident. His snarl became extremely ugly. We were all in grave danger of death.

Rage is a terrifying thing to see. That day, I saw Dad's sexual rage, and it changed my life forever. I realized nobody would be safe until he was dead. That was the moment I understood he was a murderer.

Each time Mom rejected his advances, she gave him a look of disgust. Physical fights followed. We all went into protection mode for our mom. We yelled at him to stop. Nobody could protect her. One of us crept over to the phone to call the police. We had to move sneakily. If he saw us going for the phone, he turned his attack on us.

Our small-town police officer made more than his fair share of trips to our house. It took him forever to arrive. Dad stopped attacking Mom when we told him the sheriff was on the way. He left us alone and went to the chicken house. The officer went out and talked to him. Then he came back and let us know Dad had calmed down. I can't even count how many times we called the police. We wished they would take him away!

~ Black Coffee ~

Our family home was a miniature vulture nest. The central vulture's nest was the church and community. The church nest taught us to judge, criticize, disrespect, and condemn outsiders who didn't attend our church. We also did the same harmful behavior to each other. There was no love in our home. Everyone pulled pranks on each other. Nobody cared if someone got hurt.

Sometimes my aunts and uncles came to visit and have coffee and cookies with Mom. They'd come on a Friday evening or a Saturday afternoon. They all sat at the table, sipping their *black coffee* and munching on cookies, bars, or cake. For an hour or two, they gossiped and shared everything about everyone else's lives, leaving nobody any privacy.

They talked about who had new hats, shoes, or dresses. Who did what, when, where, how, and who was dating who. They kept the gossip alive for years. Nobody could change, because gossip kept them from breaking free and becoming better. All their past mistakes hung over their heads forever.

I became increasingly appalled by the gossip as I got older. Once, after her company left, I told Mom that gossiping about everyone was hurtful. She knew it was, but she didn't stop. Gossiping is a way of life for that flock of dirty birds. *Black coffee.* Black hearts.

One Saturday, the adults were drinking coffee again. This time, my older cousin Margaret came along with her parents. Margaret rarely visited. We were all inside listening to the grown-ups. Their coffee looked quite dark on this memorable day. Margaret told some jokes and showed us some clever tricks with strings. Then she said she knew a fantastic trick. She told us to get into a line and hold hands near the electric fence. The person closest to the fence would grab it. Margaret said not to worry because nobody gets shocked. The electricity just passes through everyone. Only the last person in line would feel a slight tingling. We didn't believe her at first, but she promised it would work because she had done it before. She swore it wouldn't hurt.

We looked at Mom and Aunt Florence. We asked them whether it was true. Both of them, with a straight face, told us that if Margaret says it's true, then it's true. We agreed to try it. I said I'd be first in line because I didn't want a shock. We all lined up holding hands. I felt hesitant to grab it, but Margaret yelled not to be a fraidy-cat. She again promised that nobody would feel anything.

I grabbed the fence and received the shock of my life! I cried deeply, not just because I had received a shock, but also because three grown women had lied to us. We couldn't trust our mom after that. She didn't protect us from harm. Everyone now hated Margaret. We never believed a word she said. That was a black day for me, as those dirty birds sat there drinking their *black coffee.*

On another Saturday, when I was 14, Mom was having another coffee event. After the older girls moved out, I had to gather the eggs. I had to place them into flats that measured 1' x 1'. Each flat held 36 eggs. When the cart was full, I took all the flats to the cooler and piled them onto a table. Then, I went back out to collect more eggs.

When I finished gathering the eggs, I had to pack the flats into cases and stack them in the cooler. The egg truck came twice a week and picked them up. I did this job every day. There were also a few flats of dirty eggs I had to wash. I tried to finish my egg chores before Dad got home. However, he arrived home from work earlier on Saturdays.

I was picking eggs when he came to drive the feed cart down the aisles. Something must have put him in a terrible mood. As he drove down the aisle next to me, I felt a splash of runny chicken manure all over my legs.

Startled, I looked around. I saw Dad in the next aisle, laughing at me. My anger flared. Not only had he thrown an egg under the cages to make manure splash on me, but he was also laughing about it. I yelled, "It's not funny!" I went back to gathering eggs. Five seconds later, he threw another egg into the manure. Once more, runny chicken manure splashed all over my legs, socks, and shoes. This time, I hollered at him to knock it off! He sneered and asked, "What are you gonna do about it?" I yelled that if he didn't stop, I would throw eggs at him! Wouldn't you know, lo and behold, he did it again!

My anger boiled over. Dad had splashed manure on me for the third time. As quickly as I could, I pushed the egg cart to the end of my aisle. I ran down the aisle where he was standing on the tall feeding cart. I started throwing eggs at him from the front of his cart. All of my shots missed as he ducked behind the auger to avoid getting hit. It was of no use. I wouldn't make contact anyway. If I kept trying, one might hit him. That would mean more abuse for me later, maybe even death. I went to the house to clean up and told Mom I wasn't going back out there. Of course, all the eggs were still waiting for me the next day.

It wasn't just manure that was splattered all over me. It was also maggots. The chicken house had thousands of buzzing flies that pestered and bit my bare arms and legs. The manure attracts flies. Those flies lay trillions of eggs, which hatch into trillions of maggots. Many small white maggot worms were crawling through the manure. Sometimes, it looked like more worms than manure. It was gross.

Dad was splashing manure on me outside in the chicken house. Mom and her visitors were splashing manure on others with their gossiping inside the house. Everyone was splashing hurt, harm, and maggots onto others. How did any of them think this was right?

If God talked to my mom's preacher, why didn't He mention how harmful gossiping is to others? Her church doesn't preach any sermons about *black coffee.* They were all dirty bird vultures who wore suits, pretty hats, or fancy dresses to church. However, that made none of them any better than my dad. They were only putting lipstick on a pig. Every single one of them was splashing manure on others and shocking small children with electric fences! *Black coffee.* Black hearts.

~ Penny Pincher ~

Mom handled all the family's finances. Dad's paycheck went into the bank to pay for the bills and food. However, Mom always kept some cash on hand to buy milk and for tithing at church. She got some cash from neighbors who bought eggs and chickens from her.

Dad snuck cash from her purse, and my parents had many fights because of the missing money. Mom went to pay the neighbor for milk, and lo and behold, the money she needed was gone. She became outraged. She needed every *penny* for the family bills and to feed everyone.

My dad's earnings weren't enough to cover the family's expenses. Dad's spending money on frivolous things and stealing money from her made her angry. She hid her purse, but he always found it. Sometimes, he stole from her in the middle of the night.

Mom had to *pinch her pennies* however she could. She received government help to keep us warm and to buy food. Still, with nine girls, she had to purchase many toiletries. Those were enormous expenses for her. My mom always expressed her frustration about the girls using too many pads. We felt like we couldn't use them. Whenever we did, we felt guilty, as if we were sneaking them.

When I was 12, I babysat for a few nearby families. I earned only $1.00 to $1.50 per hour, but I purchased my own toiletries to avoid getting yelled at. However, I also knew my mom was poor and couldn't afford them.

If Mom wasn't yelling about the pads, she was yelling at us to turn off the water. To conserve water, Mom urged us not to flush the toilet unless necessary. We could use only a small amount of toilet paper.

When Dad installed the new bathroom, he messed up the plumbing. There wasn't enough water pressure for the toilet to flush properly, so it clogged often. Mom always had to pour a bucket of water into it to help it flush. We had to place soiled toilet paper in the trash can next to the toilet, which made the bathroom smell terrible.

Sometimes after a hot day of work, Mom would buy us an ice cream shake from the drive-in. On rare occasions, our parents took us out to eat at an all-you-can-eat buffet. However, it wasn't a fun outing because Dad embarrassed us by getting two heaping plates of food. Some fell onto the floor as he walked. After devouring both plates, he got two more. One kid would always make fun of him, which would often lead to a huge cursing scene. I felt like crawling under the table. I burned with embarrassment as everyone in the restaurant stared at us.

Dad took us kids fishing once a year, but we found it wasn't very fun with him yelling and cursing. We rarely caught any fish. He scared them all away. I didn't enjoy going, so I stopped. Also, I feared eating fish. When I was younger, I choked on a small bone.

The only public place we could go without him throwing a tantrum was church. Attending church was quite the dress-up event. We all pretended to be ordinary people. It was quite an act as we walked humbly up the aisle and found an empty pew. Our family filled up an entire bench.

Dad often fell asleep during the minister's 30-minute prayer and during the 1.5-hour service. He snored, and I'm sure the whole church heard him. The unfortunate boy sitting by him had to jab him with his elbow. Dad worked hard and needed the extra sleep; at least he wasn't yelling. However, I felt like hiding under the pew.

I sat next to Anna in church, but when I was 5, she left home. I then sat by Mom. She had large hands, and I entertained myself by pressing down on her protruding blood vessels. If someone started messing around, Mom gave them a *pinch.* She couldn't always reach them, so she brought her sewing needle. That day, I moved further up the pew.

I feared the needle, so I cried to Trudy and asked her if I could sit beside her. She talked to Mom, and that same evening, I sat by Trudy. She let me nap on her lap during those long sermons. I now led the family into church. I felt relieved to be away from the harm and embarrassment. As a teenager, I often napped. I slouched just right so I wouldn't fall over, as I sometimes did. I always hoped I didn't snore like Dad.

With five kids between us, Mom couldn't see me sleeping. None of my siblings could pay me enough money to give up my spot. I didn't want to get *pinched* or needled, and I was enjoying my naps.

Sometimes, we found some entertainment during those excruciatingly long services. There was an older man named Joe who used the stem of his glasses to pick his nose. We were all horrified as we watched him shove the stem halfway into his nostril. We all picked our noses, but never with anything other than our fingers — and never in church. Joe dug out his boogers in front of the entire congregation. We laughed about it on the way back home. We joked that Joe was digging for gold. No fun moment lasted long. Someone would comment about Dad's snoring. The drive then became treacherous, with Dad angry, snarling, and cursing.

Mom always cooked a big Sunday lunch. We usually had fried chicken, mashed potatoes with gravy, and a vegetable. We also had bread, which helped fill us up in case there wasn't enough food to eat. Once home, we rushed upstairs and changed into our home clothes. We had to get back to the kitchen to help prepare food and set the table.

Mom was a great cook. She made three meals every day. By mealtime, we were starving. None of us complained about the food. If we had, the person closest would have grabbed it in one fell swoop. We learned to eat fast before we lost it.

On Sundays, we had to follow a strict routine. After washing dishes, we sat at the table and did more church study. Mom read from the books that the church gave her for home lessons. They were mini-sermons. We all had to answer the questions at the end of each lesson. Mom was a staunch believer in her church's doctrine. She did her best to indoctrinate us kids, hoping we could all go to heaven.

We attended three hours of church, one hour of Sunday school, and two hours of at-home mini-sermons. We also went to catechism for an hour on Thursday evenings. Also, we had to memorize many questions and answers for Sunday school, catechism classes, and school.

The preacher gave many guilt trips about missing church. He said it was a sin unless we had a good reason. If we were sick or the roads were icy, Mom kept sermons handy to listen to at home.

The reverend said that skipping church was slapping God in the face. He portrayed God as speaking through the preacher. If we missed church, that meant we didn't want to hear what God was saying. They passed the money plate three times during each service. The deacons brought the collection pots around while we sang a song. We had to sing slowly because it took a long time for them to collect everyone's tithes. When we finished the song, the organist kept playing until the deacons returned to their seats.

When I grew bored, I stared at the money pots, wondering how much money they contained. Once, when I was 7, I kept my tithing quarter. I felt guilty all day for stealing, so I put it into the pot that evening.

The preacher led the elders and deacons out of a small consistory room at the front of the church. He shook hands with each of them as they passed him. Six elders sat in the first pew, and the six deacons had to sit in the second row. The minister stood at the bottom of the stairs and prayed in silence for five minutes. When he walked up the stairs to the pulpit, the consistory members also stopped praying and sat down. I felt relieved when church was over. They said we were horrible sinners who weren't worthy of God's love. I always left feeling sad, worthless, and afraid of God.

Sometimes, an elder and a deacon visited our home. We had to clean the house and dress up. They arrived in their church suits. They always spoke strangely, presenting themselves as reverent and holy representatives of God. We gave them high respect.

They preached a small sermon and questioned Mom about the condition of her soul. They asked about her finances, even though they already knew. She cried in embarrassment as they made her disclose her financial details in front of her children. They had no heart beneath those suits! The church forced her to have these babies with its no birth control rule. They should have given her support every month.

They made a big show of sending the deacon to their car to retrieve the checkbook. He should have had it in his pocket. They pretended to be Santa Claus as they wrote her a check. They have no shame! She had 15 children, and they only gave her enough money to help her for a couple of months.

Before leaving, they prayed for God to save our souls. They told us God commands us to replenish the earth. They said God gives us as many children as He predestined for us. However, they *pinched their pennies* when it came to supporting those kids. Mom had to contact them twice a year for help. Mom's financial burden was enormous. She had to raise 15 children on very little money.

Many of those guys pretended to be a holy-Joe. My brother, Ben, was friends with Elder Harry's son. He went to his house once and told us that Elder Harry cussed like a sailor. He was always angry and yelling at his kids. I felt sick knowing that this "holy man of God" was only pretending to be holy on Sundays.

We had nothing extra. We didn't have air conditioning until I was 13 years old. One of the older kids gave Mom a window air conditioner. All of us were a ragged mess. We all wore hand-me-downs and clothes given to us by a kind lady from church. After I earned money of my own, I could buy some new clothes.

Mom's church didn't celebrate Christmas with gifts, trees, or decorations. On Christmas, we had a church service and dinner at home. One year around Christmas, Dad's work gave us kids a gift. I received a new pair of pajamas. Otherwise, Mom *pinched her pennies* so we could survive.

~ Deviled Eggs ~

When Anna, Ella, and Jerry were young, Mom read them a poem repeatedly. "Which Loved Best?" was their daily lesson. The poem said that the child who helps their mother the most is the one who loves their mother the best. In the poem, Fan was the best little helper. John didn't help at all, and Nell helped, but spent the day pouting. Her mother was glad when Nell went out to play.

Mom and my three oldest siblings became programmed by the repetition of this poem. They became who the poem told them to be. Mom pitted each child against the other with the brainwashing of this simple poem.

Jerry grew up to be Little John. He never helped his mother; instead, he rushed outside to play. Anna became Little Fan. It became a competition for her to prove that she was her mother's best helper. Little Fan was a special child who loved her mother the most. She happily helped with the baby and all the household chores.

Ella became Nell. She spent the day pouting. Ella had every reason to pout and cry. She endured severe abuse from the moment of her birth until she left home.

Anna helped with changing diapers, giving baths, feeding, and putting us to bed. As the number of mouths to feed grew, Anna's workload increased. She was Mom's nursemaid. She was Little Fan! She was under massive pressure and stress.

Anna became overwhelmed by the tremendous amount of work. With many babies underfoot, she delegated the household, gardening, and chicken coop chores to the other children. She made sure everyone finished their chores correctly and on time. Anna was the boss. She was second in command to our mom.

Ella and Peggy grew resentful, not wanting Anna to tell them what to do. They couldn't understand the burden placed on Little Fan's shoulders. She was the best helper who pleased her mother the most. Little Fan would do anything to stay in her mother's good graces. They didn't understand that Little Fan loved Mother best.

When Ella wasn't working fast enough and Peggy became rebellious, fights broke out. Sometimes Anna hit them with the broom. Little Fan always had the broom. It was her job to sweep and keep everything tidy. Why couldn't Ella and Peggy get it through their thick skulls that this is how we love our mother the best?

We all drank baby formula, which upset our stomachs. We were all fussy babies and cried a lot. All of us experienced womb trauma. We heard all the anger and fighting before we were even born.

Ella was slow in doing her work. She was enduring much abuse and became a complete basket case. If Dad and Jerry weren't hurting her, then Mom and Anna were hollering at her to work faster or redo it because it wasn't right. The tears Ella cried could fill an ocean.

Peggy talked back and became sassy, loud, and mouthy. If Dad were around when fights broke out, he would grab

Peggy and bash her head against the wall. Once, he smashed her head so hard that it left a massive hole in the wall.

Another time, Dad threw a large metal toy truck at Peggy. It hit her on the head, causing a big gash. Blood gushed down her face. Once, when Peggy was by the stove cooking, she fainted and collapsed. It might have stemmed from anxiety and stress. Otherwise, it was head trauma because of Dad abusing her.

Peggy lashed out at everyone around her. She did sloppy work on purpose, which made Anna angry. Peggy didn't care. If anyone chastised her, they paid for it with her sharp tongue.

Peggy decided she needed a partner in crime. She took Jolene under her wing. Together, they plotted to stand up against Dad and rebel against Mom. They were always looking for a fight. During mealtime, they sat together and whispered to each other in an odd, passive-aggressive manner. They held their hand near their mouth as if to whisper. They twisted one corner of their mouths downward and to the side. Then they made an out-loud, snide comment about someone.

Their voices sounded weird because their mouths were twisted and mostly closed. Everyone could hear what they said. They intended their target to hear them. They often did this pretend-whisper talk with each other. However, they also did this ridiculous-looking, out-loud, fake whisper to anyone nearby. Their primary target was Dad, but we all got some of their trash talk. Anytime we heard Peggy's loud, unpleasant, cackling laugh, we knew they were being cruel to someone.

Jolene became Peggy's protégé. Their loudmouth, sassy, and rebellious attitude brought more trouble for us kids. They stirred the pot whenever they could. Dad always aimed to hurt them. They hated Dad, and Dad hated them.

Jolene, in her rebellion, started wearing pants and makeup. She listened to music that Mom didn't allow us to listen to. The older girls bore the brunt of Mom's anger. They rebelled without caring about the consequences. They broke Mom in, which made it easier for us younger girls as we got older. When I began wearing makeup to school, a teacher approached me and said I had to remove it. I wore less after that and hoped she wouldn't notice.

There were many *devils* in our home. They tore our innocence from us, once tender and precious babies. What they poured into our empty shells was fear, abuse, pain, anger, and hate.

Surprisingly, Ella escaped our house alive. As the girls grew older, they began dating, which is how Ella met Charles. Ella told him about her abuse. Charles came to the house and yelled at my parents. He insisted they stop hurting Ella. They told Charles that Ella was worthless and lazy. Charles said that if they don't want Ella, then he would take her off their hands. My parents replied, "Fine, take her!" Charles commanded Ella to grab her belongings, and that was it. Ella was gone — right then, and right there!

Ella and Charles eloped and moved far away. I don't believe anyone can truly escape, given what she endured. Ella struggled with depression and PTSD for many years. After some years, she found peace through her relationship with our Heavenly Father, who comforted her heart.

Peggy and Jolene were defiant and refused to accept the same abuse Ella had endured. They were determined to protect themselves. The more vicious they got, the more ferocious our dad became. It was a never-ending cycle. We all wanted these two girls to stop causing strife. Every time they stirred the pot, Dad blew a gasket, and the roof came crashing down. The devil was among us. Abuse was our soup each day. Our house was without love. It was filled with *deviled eggs* that had shells in their yolks.

Mom's church taught us to fear the devil. They portrayed him as hiding behind every bush and just around the corner. They said he tempted everyone to do evil and was gathering souls to take to hell with him.

I always feared that the devil could read my mind. I didn't dare say or think bad things about him because I worried he'd be mad and drag me to hell. The last thing I wanted was to burn forever. Fearing he was under my bed, I ran fast and jumped into bed so he wouldn't snatch me. The church also made us terrified of God. They said He becomes angry and throws disobedient children into a forever-burning fire in hell. They didn't realize our home was already a living hell.

~ Angel Wings ~

When I was a baby, Anna told Peggy to change my diaper. Peggy left me unattended, and I fell off the tall diaper-changing table. One of the plastic drawer handles had broken in half, exposing its sharp inner edges. As I rolled off the table, my cheek scraped against the sharp handle. My face received a severe cut, and I had to get stitches.

After this incident, Anna took on my care and nurturing. I became her baby. She might have felt guilty for handing my care over to Peggy. After that, Anna assigned Trudy to help with the babies. Peggy was not responsible enough.

With so much to do, Anna never had a childhood. She was always busy taking care of babies, cooking, and cleaning. If she went to read her book, Mom hollered at her to get back downstairs.

Anna became my mommy. She took me under her wing. Anna was my Nana. I slept with her, and I grew to love her as if she were my mother. She loved me as if I were her own baby. I missed her when she was at school. She also worked at the newspaper office on Saturdays. I looked forward to her coming home. I ran out to meet her and told her everything that had happened while she was away. If anyone had been cruel to me, I tattled on them, and she took care of it.

I loved sleeping and snuggling with her. She was the best person in the entire world. She bought me a birthday cake. It was beautiful! Nobody had ever received a cake before! Wow! My Nana loved me so much! I was so thankful that she was protecting and comforting me.

Even though Dad always made threats to kill us, Nana kept me safe. Once, when she was sweeping the floor, Dad became angry and threw a massive temper tantrum. Nana shouted at him and said, "You had better sit down and shut up or I'm gonna run you through with this broom!" Wow! He sat down! She protected me every night. We pushed a heavy dresser against our bedroom door while we slept so he couldn't get in. I felt so safe with her.

Then, one dreadful day when I was five, Nana took me upstairs to our room. She sat beside me on our bed and took my hand in hers. Her voice sounded bleak as she told me she was leaving home. She was moving out to live with her friend. I hesitantly asked if I could go with her. We both started crying as she told me no. She explained why I couldn't go. Nothing she said made any sense. This could not be happening! This could not be real! She said she was moving in a couple of days. I've never cried so hard. No, Nana! Please don't go away! Please don't leave me here alone! I'll be afraid if you're not here. There will be no one to protect me. Who will take care of me? Who will love me? No! Please, no!

Over the next few days, I looked for every chance to change her mind. I begged, I pleaded, and I cried. I felt so sad. My tears wouldn't stop! I needed her to stay, and if she couldn't, I wanted to go with her. I was losing my Nana.

On the day she left, she took me outside and had me choose a kitten from a recent litter. She said a kitty would help comfort me. Through my tears and my sobbing, I picked out a beautiful, fluffy, light orange and white kitten. Nana helped me give my new little kitty a name. We named her Puff. I held Puff close to my chest. As tears streamed down my face, I watched my mommy leave our big, scary chicken farm.

My sadness and pain were overwhelming. My heart felt broken. A knife was stabbing me from the inside. I felt abandoned and alone. She left me! I cried endlessly. I spent all my time cuddling with Puff. Mom barely got me into the house for dinner. My heart felt shattered. I was finding comfort in my sweet baby kitty. I was hiding from all the hurtful people inside that house. My protector was gone. Nana was gone. My *angel wings* were gone.

Then, one day, I heard Anna was coming to visit with her new husband. I was excited and watched the end of the driveway for her to arrive. Finally, she came. I ran to hug her. Her visit only brought me more tears. My Nana was acting differently now with this new man around her. She wasn't here to see me. They were here to have a serious grown-up visit with Mom.

They talked to Mom about the abuse happening in our home. This man sounded gruff, and I felt scared to be around him. Nana told us kids to stay outside. When they finished talking to Mom, they left right away. She hugged me and said goodbye. I watched tearfully as Nana left with that scary man. She waved to me with tears in her eyes as they drove off down the driveway.

I didn't get what I had hoped for. My Nana wasn't coming back. Sinking deeper into sadness, I withdrew from everything and everyone around me. The only joy I had was my baby Puff. I spent every spare moment with her. I had to protect my kitty from my dad and brothers. When they saw me with Puff, they made mean and jealous comments. They even made death threats toward my kitty. I knew that one of them would hurt her. They always hurt, shot, and kicked animals.

~ Puff ~

Dread filled my heart one morning as I went outside to find my kitty. Puff was nowhere to be found. I searched for her all day. I asked everyone if they had seen her, even asking my brothers a few times if they had done something to her. Everyone denied having seen her. I cried all day while searching for her. Eventually, I had to go to bed, but I continued searching every day, hoping she would return. Nana had given her to me. Puff was all I had left of my Nana. I couldn't find Puff. She was gone. My heart felt shattered again!

My memory is clouded because of the trauma. Still, I remember one day, after I had stopped searching for Puff, one boy, out of the blue, mentioned that I should look for Puff under the tool shed. I could tell from their tone that they knew she was there. I ran and looked. There, under the shed, way in the back, lay my sweet baby Puff. She was dead. My heart broke into a million pieces. I knew they had killed her and thrown her under there. The cruelty, jealousy, and hatred were so rampant at our house. I lay by that shed crying for hours. Everyone I loved seemed to be going up in a *puff of smoke.* I never found out who did this horrible thing to my little Puff. It could have been any of them.

My mom must have sensed my pain. A few years later, she brought a cat home from someone at her work. It was a white and orange indoor cat, spayed and declawed. I claimed Tiger right away. Now, I had a new best friend. I protected her fiercely. If anyone was mean to her, I screamed at them. They all knew I would die for this kitty. After witnessing my grief over little Puff, they knew deep down in their souls that nobody could hurt Tiger and live to tell about it.

~ Double Yolks ~

Mom's church excommunicated Anna because she had married a divorced man. The *yolk* will ultimately be on them. After her marriage, we called her when a fight broke out at our house. We thought her husband, Jake, could help protect us from Dad. They came several times, but then we stopped calling her. Jake brought even more fighting into our home. We experienced two episodes of fear instead of just one with Dad.

I missed my Nana. Sometimes, she brought me to her house. I felt scared of Jake and stayed quiet when he was around. He was sometimes mean to Anna and their little kids. I no longer knew where I fit in her life.

When her oldest daughter, Marrianne, was 5 years old, Jake had a farm machinery accident and died. Anna felt sad, so Mom let me visit her more often. Anna found another husband. She *yoked* up again, but I also felt afraid of him. I became worried when he was cruel to Anna's kids. He did not harm me, but I didn't feel comfortable around him.

I continued to visit my Nana occasionally, but as I began babysitting and dating, I went to her house less frequently. She had a life of her own. Sometimes, there were just as many fights at her home as at mine. It was easier to babysit with no fights. I experienced love from Nana, so I saw that there was an opposite to all the hate. I just had to find it, but I didn't know how.

~ Slaughtered Chicks ~

Every spring, Mom bought hundreds of baby *chicks* to raise for food. These chicks were so cute and cuddly. We placed them in a small shed under heat lamps. As the weather warmed up and the chicks grew larger, we moved them to a bigger shed. When they became full grown, we butchered them for food.

The butchering process entailed one person holding the chicken's feet and wings together. Another person held its head onto a wooden board and chopped off its head with a hatchet. They tossed the chicken out onto the grass. The chickens jumped and flopped, with blood squirting out of their necks. It took them a few minutes to bleed out. Then, we took the dead chickens and either skinned them or plucked their feathers.

We removed all the guts, keeping only the necks, gizzards, hearts, and livers. Butchering chickens was a family affair. Everyone helped, except for my dad, who was at work. We didn't want his help. The hatchet was an easy weapon for him to wield. We had to keep him away from it. The kids did all the gutting, skinning, and feathering. Mom washed, cut, and packaged them.

Mom filled our freezer with chickens and sold some to neighbors. Every summer, we spent many days going through this bloody, slimy process. It provided us with food for the year. We ate chicken often. Mom had learned in her childhood how to keep us fed throughout the year.

Once, as we were finishing our last chicken, we heard a gunshot. I felt a sharp sting on my forehead. I didn't know what had hit me. We all looked toward the house and saw my brother Ben holding a shotgun. I was furious because a BB from his spray hit me. He could have killed us. My brothers did reckless and dangerous things. They had too much extra time. We girls worked ourselves half to death, while they seemed to create more work with their destructiveness.

July 4 was a dangerous day. The boys went wild and did foolish and risky things with fireworks. It was safer to stay indoors. Otherwise, we would have gotten hurt because of their negligence. They acted recklessly on motorcycles and go-karts. Someone always got hurt. When they got a car, it was nothing but screeching tires and revving engines. They were complete motor-heads.

My brothers were under my dad's wing, doing outside chores with him. They spent much of their time fixing their motor toys. The girls did all the cooking, dishes, cleaning, gardening, food storage, laundry, and most of the chicken house chores. We had to gather all the eggs into flats, wash the dirty eggs, and box them into the egg cooler. When the truck arrived to pick up the eggs, I helped the guy load the cases into his truck. Sometimes, he gave me a quarter. It seemed like a lot of money at the time. When he stopped having quarters in his pocket, I stopped helping.

The boys had some outdoor chores. Sometimes, they hooked up the manure spreader to the tractor and spread chicken manure onto the neighbor's field. Every Saturday, they chained the garden tractor to a large, heavy metal scraper. With a wide shovel, I pushed the manure over to the scraper. My brothers pulled the manure to the auger trough system, which then carried it outside.

In time, I had to maneuver the heavy scraper and garden tractor as well. After Harlan and Ben moved out, my two younger brothers, Jesse and Pete, had to help me clean the manure. One day, while trying to bang the sticky chicken manure off the scraper, I accidentally slammed it down on my big toe. My toenail got shattered. I barely made it to the house because of the severe pain. The boys helped me hobble as blood seeped through my shoe. I sat on the bathroom counter to put my toe under water. I could hardly get my sock off because of the excruciating pain.

After removing my sock, I noticed I had toenail polish on. Mom worked nights, so she was still asleep that morning. We couldn't wake her for help until I removed the polish. It was against church rules to wear any makeup. I told Pete to run upstairs and grab my polish remover. I took the polish off four toes. However, there was no way on God's green earth that I could touch my big toe. I had to wake Mom up, polish and all. Surprisingly, she said nothing about the polish. However, I knew she believed God had punished me for wearing toenail polish.

When my youngest brother, Alex, was seven, he climbed onto the tractor. He opened the gas cap to siphon gas from the tank. After smelling and drinking some gas, he fainted and fell to the ground. He was never the same after that. Massive damage had been done. He had to attend a school for children with learning disabilities. Our farm was a circus with 17 clowns.

Being under Dad's wing, my brothers often hung out with him in the chicken house cooler. They drank beer and smoked cigarettes. Dad was a nasty man and taught my brothers to be abusive, crude, and vulgar. He showed them how to cuss, lie, cheat, and steal, as well as to be disrespectful, careless, and wild.

Dad abused the boys by teaching them about intimacy and sharing pornography with them at a young age. He disrespected women, comparing them to cows, and said they were only suitable for breeding, cooking, and housework.

Our dad and brothers abused us all with their vulgar slang and innuendos. We all endured sexual abuse in one form or another. We all had to hear our parents fighting about intimacy. Every day, he called us derogatory names. He snarled and called us a female or a heifer. He always threatened to run us through with a screwdriver, a pitchfork, or a knife. We were merely baby *chicks* who didn't deserve his *slaughter.*

We tried to stay away from Dad as much as possible. However, we couldn't escape his vulgar and angry words. If we got near him, we were at risk of being shoved, pushed, hit, or kicked. We feared for our lives from morning until night.

Mom's church portrayed that women are inferior to men. They said God created women to be the man's helper. Only men could serve as ministers, elders, and deacons. Women were to remain silent and discuss church matters with their husbands when they got home. Surprisingly, women could play the organ during services. However, the layout was such that the congregation couldn't see the organist. Women could volunteer for nursery duty. The nursery was in the basement so that the children wouldn't disrupt the sermon.

There were loudspeakers in the nursery. The children had to be kept quiet so the women could listen to the sermon. Nobody could talk. They said the entire building was God's sanctuary. We could only nod hello to people as we walked by them.

Women were required to be submissive to their husbands. The preacher didn't talk about intimacy. However, when he preached sermons about submitting to one's husband, it also applied to romantic relationships. The women endured extreme levels of suppression and servitude. These pompous men wanted the women to serve, bow down to, and worship them.

Nobody could address the minister as a preacher. He had to be addressed as Reverend. He was to be revered as the "man of God." Mom's church didn't believe that God used women as preachers or prophetesses. They portrayed God as thinking more highly of and speaking only through men.

~ Carrot Tops ~

Many unimaginable and horrifying things happened on that chicken farm. One morning, my older sister, Susan, came running in from outside, screaming and crying. Someone had killed all of her rabbits during the night. She headed straight for Dad with every intention of killing him. She was screaming at him that he had killed her bunnies. Oh, no! She had 20 bunny rabbits. They were her babies. She cared for them, always feeding them *carrot tops* and any vegetable scraps they'd eat. Susan spent hours outside with her fur balls, nurturing and caring for them.

Dad, being a large man, warded her off. We all ran outside and saw her bunnies scattered dead on the ground. In trying to figure out how this happened, one kid suggested a fox may have done it. Another kid said a fox would have eaten them. Susan showed us that only a human could unlock the cages. Someone else pointed out that the bunnies had no blood on them. Susan held up a bunny to show us how its head flopped from side to side. We realized that someone had snapped their necks.

Many times, Dad threatened to do these kinds of horrific things. He told Susan before that he would hurt or kill her bunnies. No! He didn't do this! This is not happening! How could someone be so cruel? We were all crying and sad.

Dad denied killing Susan's bunnies. He claimed that the red-headed guy in the barn attic did it. Dad was a liar, and we all suspected him of it. Still, his denial made us wonder. Maybe the stranger in our barn did commit this massacre. Susan's devastating loss changed her forever. Nobody can experience a horrendous trauma such as this without jumping into the pan of scrambled eggs.

A few months prior, Carrot Top gave us his reign of terror. We played outside in the abandoned buildings. One afternoon, Jolene was standing by the kitchen window, which faced the barn. Suddenly, she screamed that a red-haired guy had come out of our barn and was crossing the field toward town.

Everyone rushed to look. A tremendous wave of fear swept over us. Why was this *carrot-top* man in our barn? Had he been sleeping there? Would he come back? The attic had some hay bales. He might be using that for bedding. The older kids went and searched the barn. They found signs that this man was using the attic as his sleeping quarters.

Was he the guy who had escaped from jail? We didn't know, but we did know he had stolen our safe place to play — our spot we went to escape the abusive home we lived in. We felt afraid of going down there now.

After avoiding the barn for a month, we found the courage to reclaim what was ours. Carrot Top had to be gone by now. We felt hesitant as we made our way down there. Each dared the other to go in first.

We spent an hour shaking sticks, yelling, and making loud noises at the imposter. None of us dared to enter. The following week, we played near the barn. We hoped our noise would scare the intruder away, if he were still there. The boys called him names and acted tough and brave.

Eventually, we decided to all go in together. We all grabbed our weapons — a stick or a metal bar, whatever we could find to defend ourselves. Before entering, we all shouted at him, warning that we were coming in. We hollered that he had best leave, because if he were still in there, we would deal with him.

When we finally went in, we moved slowly and quietly. We wanted to hear whether Carrot Top was still there. We all had our forefingers on our lips to shush each other. Everyone tried not to step on anything to avoid making noise. Suddenly, we heard squeaking from the rafters. He was walking above us. We all froze. Our jaws hit the floor, and our eyes almost popped out of their sockets. We raced back to the house in fear for our lives.

After some weeks, Ben devised a plan to sneak in quietly this time, so Carrot Top wouldn't know we were there. Ben said he felt brave enough to peek into the attic. We went ahead with the plan. Without a noise, we walked down to the barn. Again, everyone held a finger to their lips as we entered. The ladder was at the back. As we tiptoed in that direction, we kept our eyes and ears peeled. We were ready to run!

When we reached the ladder, we all stood as quiet as mice while Ben worked up his nerve. We didn't hear any squeaking. We assumed the impostor wasn't up there this time. After lots of silent arm-waving from us, Ben slowly started up the ladder. At a snail's pace, he climbed a couple of rungs at a time. As he peeked into the attic, he abruptly scrambled back down. He started running and shouted for everyone to run! We sprinted back to the house. Ben looked as pale as a ghost. He said he saw something moving. He swore it was the guy.

We weren't sure whether Ben was telling the truth. We accused him of feeling scared and of making up a story to avoid going up. After a few weeks, we made another plan to confront the bully. We were determined to scare this intruder away. This time, Harlan and Ben grabbed their shotguns. We boldly marched down to the barn.

As we entered, we stopped dead in our tracks. The sight of it will never leave my mind. Hanging from the ceiling was a perfectly tied noose. It was a brand-new rope, made specifically to hang us to death. Our jaws hit the floor, and our eyes popped out of their sockets. None of us said a word. We all ran back to the house. The message was clear. We all knew our safe place was gone forever!

Carrot Top had won. It was a terrifying and heartbreaking day. We were now forced to face the terrible things happening inside the house. Dad stole our safety inside our home, and now the red-headed guy in the barn attic had stolen our outside play place.

It's possible that this intruder killed Susan's bunnies. We never found out the truth. If Dad did it, he wouldn't have admitted it. He knew Susan would have killed him. He became afraid of Susan that day as she endured the greatest loss of her life. She threatened his life many times over if she ever learned that he had slaughtered her bunnies.

Looking back, I don't know why Mom didn't call the police. She probably thought we bothered them enough by calling them out for Dad. When Jerry came to visit, she had him remove the noose. A couple of years later, Mom had the fire department burn the barn. It was old and falling apart.

We cried many tears as we endured many losses. Many terrible people were doing many horrible things. How does anyone get into the pan of sunny-side-up?

~ Muddy Pigs ~

Before Mom's church built a private school, we attended public school. We girls felt out of place wearing skirts while the other girls wore pants. When I was in kindergarten, I was too shy to ask to go to the bathroom. I tried to hold it, but had an accident at my desk. Utterly embarrassed, I didn't know what to do and stayed seated while the kids went to recess.

My teacher was kind and took me to the nurse's office. They helped me get cleaned up. They had an extra pair of pants. That was a no-no for Mom. I was terrified to get on the bus. Not only would my siblings see me wearing pants, but they would make a big deal about it in front of everyone. Luckily, I thought about lying when they asked. I said my skirt got dirty during recess. When I got home, I quickly changed into a skirt before Mom could ask questions.

I didn't have any friends during the few years of public school. I felt embarrassed about wearing skirts. Mom said that people who wore pants were gentiles and destined for hell. She was strict about the church rules. We couldn't have a television. We also couldn't watch television at school, even if the teacher used it for educational purposes or to play a movie as a reward for good behavior.

When I was in first grade, my teacher started a movie. She came over and told me that my mom didn't want me watching it. She said Mom requested I put my head down on the desk. I felt mortified. My classmates likely thought I was a freak.

In second grade, I pretended I was sick so I could skip school. During the morning, I started horsing around and didn't look sick. Mom told Ella to take me to school. On the way, I begged Ella not to tell my teacher I wasn't sick. To my relief, she told my teacher that I was feeling better.

When I entered third grade, we started attending the church's private school. Amy, a girl in my class, also rode my bus. We sat together and played during recess. Most of third grade was fun. All the girls wore dresses, so I didn't feel like an outsider. The teacher was friendly. The entire class played nicely on the playground.

I got head lice from a girl this year, which led to severe abuse at home. Susan shunned me for an entire year. My mom treated my head and bedding to remove the lice, but Susan became cruel to me. She called me names and implied that I was dirty. She wanted me to stay far away from her.

Susan sat opposite me at dinner on purpose. The girls all had to sleep together in the large bedroom upstairs. Although Susan was in a completely different bed across the room, she began wearing a winter stocking hat to bed. She tucked her hair inside to avoid getting head lice from me. She wore this yellow hat for over a year!

Whenever I got close to Susan, she made a harsh remark to get away from her so she wouldn't catch my bugs. She looked at me with disgust. She wanted me to know that she thought I was a cesspool. Susan avoided being anywhere near me.

I can't recall my fourth-grade year well. During the first week of school, Amy approached me. She accused me of stealing her wallet on the bus. I told her I didn't steal it, but she wouldn't listen. She turned up her nose and walked away. Amy told everyone in our class and turned them all against me with her false accusations. The entire fourth grade was a blur because I had no one to play with during recess. I sat alone on the swings while they all treated me as if I were an evil thief. The teachers weren't helpful. They didn't know what was happening to me, and I was too shy to tell them. It was a sad year.

Before school, everyone in all grades played on the playground. I tried to go by my older siblings, who were on the sling-swing, but that almost got me killed. It was a tall pole with ten long chains hanging from the top. Each chain had a handle. We held the handle and ran around the pole. The faster everyone ran, the farther each person sailed through the air. It felt safe for this purpose, but it became dangerous when they wrapped one chain around all the others on the pole, which made one kid fly high into the air.

They put me on the sling-swing. I soared high. My body was straight out from the top of the pole. I lost my grip and fell to the ground. I got bruised up pretty badly, but had no broken bones. They all laughed, thinking it was the funniest thing ever. I went back to my swing and stayed away from those rough older kids.

When fifth grade began, Amy apologized for accusing me of stealing her wallet. She said she found it in her little sister's toy box. I was glad to receive an apology, but the damage had been done. She didn't tell the kids in our class that I wasn't guilty, so some students continued being cruel to me. Nick was especially mean. When standing in line behind me, he kicked his foot against the back of my knee to make my leg give out. He would also hit my funny bone with his book.

Although I had received an apology, and Amy wasn't being mean anymore, fifth grade still felt embarrassing. My teacher that year was Mr. Johnson. He had been my brother Ben's teacher the previous year. Ben was one grade ahead of me. He was an unruly kid and didn't like Mr. Johnson because he punished him for his bad behavior. Before caller ID existed, my brothers often got away with making prank phone calls. Mr. Johnson was at the top of Harlan and Ben's prank-calling list. Whenever Mom went to the chicken coop or ran errands, Harlan and Ben would grab the phone and make prank calls to my teacher.

One day at school, Ben foolishly asked Mr. Johnson if he had received any phone calls lately. Of course, the police arrived at our house. How embarrassing. For the entire year, I didn't dare look at or speak to my teacher.

Once, I snuck some chewing gum to school. It somehow got in my hair! I had to tell Mr. Johnson I needed help. He sent me to the secretary, who spent an hour removing the gum from my hair.

Ben eventually got expelled from school. He always caused trouble, pulled pranks, and became rebellious and destructive. He disrupted class more days than not. Ben served many full days of detention in the storage area above the gymnasium and also received detention after school. When he was in eleventh grade, the school principal was scolding him. Ben wound up and punched him in the face. He knocked him out cold. The principal immediately expelled Ben, and he could never return to school. Ben was a big farm boy, so I'm surprised that the principal wasn't seriously hurt.

At the start of sixth grade, I began using my sister's hand-me-down purse. All the girls now carried purses, and I wanted one too. I searched for items to put in my new purse. Mom had a small bottle of baby powder she had gotten from the hospital. She said I could have it.

Nick rode my bus. One morning, he grabbed my purse. I tried getting it back, but he put it on the floor. I ignored him and pretended he wasn't upsetting me. I thought he would return it when we got off the bus. If he didn't, I'd tell the teacher. Nick dug through my belongings. When he found the baby powder, he went ballistic. He acted horrified and scornfully started yelling, "Baby Powder! Baby Powder!"

Nick returned my purse, but he kept the baby powder. He showed it to all the boys in our class before school started. Throughout sixth grade, every boy called me "Baby Powder" every chance they got.

The school hired a new teacher named Mr. Baker. He also served as a counselor. My mom began seeing him for therapy. He recommended to Mom that we kids see him, too. She arranged for us to meet him during school hours. I felt ashamed about going to a therapist, especially since I had to get up in the middle of class. As I walked past the boys in my row of desks, they whispered "Baby Powder" at me.

It wasn't easy talking to the counselor. I said nothing other than that I was doing fine. If I had spoken about the abuse at home, I would have fallen apart. I didn't want to cry in front of a stranger. One day, as I was leaving class, Brian stuck his foot out to trip me as I walked past his desk. The counselor could tell I felt upset. I told him that the boys were calling me names, and that one boy had tried to make me fall today. The counselor must have spoken with them because, thankfully, they stopped saying "Baby Powder," and Brian never tripped me again.

After sixth grade, I had a choice to continue seeing the counselor, but I decided not to. I didn't feel comfortable with him, and it was embarrassing to leave class to see a therapist.

In seventh grade, we started using lockers and switching classrooms for each subject. Home economics was fun because we learned to sew and cook. I also took a shop class for one semester. A lanky boy named Tom always ran up and kicked me in the hallway between classes. I tolerated his behavior for the entire year. I was always on high alert, but he often caught me off guard. A teacher saw him do it once, and they began supervising the hallway where Tom was kicking me.

I had a terrible experience in eighth grade. The previous year, I helped the teachers by running errands and copying papers at the office. On Monday nights, Mom attended adult choir practice at the school. They got together to sing hymns and socialize. Sometimes, I went with her. Dana and Nicole also came with their parents. They were in my younger sister Danielle's seventh-grade class. I didn't hang out with them. I wandered the halls or stayed in the music room, listening to the adults sing.

Once, the girls approached me and asked if I knew how to use the copy machine. I told them I did. They asked me to show them how to operate it. They had taken a test from Mr. Baker's desk and wanted a copy to study. I felt hesitant. However, they insisted, "Only this one time," and "Nobody will ever know." I gave in because these girls were vindictive. If I didn't help them, I might face their repercussions. They could make things difficult for me at school with their haughty, condescending cruelty. I agreed to help them, but only this once.

A few days later, Dana rushed over to me as school was letting out. She told me that Mr. Baker had found out they had cheated. She said they told him I had shown them how to make copies. My heart sank deep into my stomach as embarrassment and fear started pounding in my chest. I quickly left and got on the bus so he couldn't question me.

Feeling sick to my stomach, knowing that Mr. Baker knew that I had helped them, I never wanted to show my face at school again. I stayed home pretending to be sick for three whole days. Unable to skip school forever, I gathered the courage to go back. I hoped he wasn't mad at me. I naively hoped that he had forgotten about it.

That wasn't the case. After class, he asked me to stay back. He inquired about helping those girls make copies. I admitted that I had shown them how to do it. He asked if I knew what they were copying, and I admitted I did.

Mr. Baker expressed his deep displeasure with me. Before he let me leave, he told me, "I'll forgive you, but I'll never forget." Wow! My heart felt crushed. Even though he wasn't my friend, I left his room feeling like I had just lost a friend. I went to him for counseling in sixth grade. I knew that if I had an emergency, I could go to him for help. However, that door had now slammed shut. When he said he would never forget, I felt like this one mistake would hang over my head forever. He didn't ask me why I had done it. Maybe he did, but I didn't understand why at the time. It may have been too hard to explain.

~ Snakes in the Garden ~

High school was a blur. I started dating. However, I was always dating a bunch of *snakes.* My first boyfriend, Ken, was a friend of my brother's. He was quite unattractive, but I wanted to get out of the house. Dating him gave me that chance. We were together for about six months. One day, out of the blue, Harlan told me Ken was breaking up with me. He wouldn't say why.

I felt hurt, of course. What would make this ugly guy break up with me? I figured it out when Harlan was talking to Ken on the phone. They were making plans for that evening. I insisted that Harlan ask him why. The reason he gave me was that I wouldn't be intimate with Ken. The words Ken used were much more vulgar. What Harlan told me shocked me to my core. What a *snake!*

I met my second boyfriend, Craig, at a Youth Day event. The church organized it for us to enjoy outdoor fun and games. Craig attended a nearby Calvinist church. He and his brother came to join in the fun. Craig, too, wasn't good-looking. However, he was a boy who showed an interest in me, and I was a teenage girl looking for a boyfriend.

Craig was self-absorbed and conceited. He was cocky and demanding. I wasn't able to keep telling him no to intimacy. He was forceful and eager to add another girl to his list. I didn't like him much. I thought he disrespected his mother.

One Saturday, my siblings and I went snow sledding at a popular snow hill. We used a giant inner tube from a tractor tire. I invited Craig to meet us there. It wasn't fun, as he spent half the day moping in his car. He said I acted like I didn't want to spend time with him, and he was right. He was a fuddy-duddy. Whenever I asked if he wanted to get on the tube, he refused. Then, he got mad at me for going without him.

The last ride down the hill turned treacherous for me. All ten of us crammed onto the tube and off we went. Suddenly, everyone started screaming and jumping off. I had my back toward the bottom of the hill, so I couldn't see why they were panicking. Before I could look, I slammed right into a giant tree. I lay there crying and in tremendous pain. It took forever for my siblings to help me up the hill. When we reached the top, I sat on the ground, not knowing how to make the terrible pain in my ribs stop.

Ben went and told Craig what had happened. He came over, but he didn't ask if I was okay. We didn't have cell phones back then. We couldn't call a hospital or an ambulance. After a while, Harlan decided we should go to Peggy's house to call Mom. Her husband, Kevin, was out sledding with us. He said that was fine. Craig couldn't believe my pain was so bad that I couldn't get up. He snapped at me, saying, "Come on, get up! Quit faking it. You aren't hurt that badly!" I could barely get into the car. When we got to Peggy's, I stayed put while she called Mom and asked what to do. Mom told her to bring me to the hospital, and she would tell them we are on our way.

Craig drove me there. It was a half-hour trip. As we passed the doctor's office on Main Street, he was certain that was where we needed to go. I walked from the parking lot to the door, only to find it closed. In much pain, I hobbled back to the car with no help from Craig.

Craig got me to the right hospital, but he wouldn't come in with me. He said he felt embarrassed about my getting hurt so stupidly. He was talking down to me and shunning me for getting hurt. Later, after I had X-rays, they settled me into a hospital room with two broken ribs. Craig eventually came in to tell me he was going home and would see me tomorrow.

The hospital kept me overnight to make sure that the broken ribs hadn't injured my spleen. When Craig came the next day, he brought a bag of candy. As he handed it to me, he acted as if I should bow down to him for the gift. He didn't stay long. Mom arrived to take me home. After I got settled at home, I ended the relationship with Craig. He was cruel and too embarrassed to go into the emergency room with me when I needed serious care. I hope he never found a wife. That poor woman would suffer a miserable life with such a *snake.*

The next boyfriend I had was Keith. My sister, Jolene, was dating his brother, Dennis. They arranged for me to meet Keith. He was a tall, skinny guy with an unusual bowl-shaped haircut. He wasn't good-looking, but he was better than the others. I dated him for over a year.

Surprisingly, all of us girls could babysit to earn money. Most of the families had a TV, so we wanted to babysit for them. It was a relief to get out of our abusive home and relax with some TV.

Sometimes, Keith came over to the house where I was babysitting. He seemed oddly shy. He was embarrassed to go out in public, and he always acted awkwardly. His face often turned red from embarrassment.

While dating Keith, I ended up in the hospital with an eating disorder. He told me on the phone that he wasn't coming to visit. He said he felt embarrassed because of why I was there. Another *snake!* I told him that if he didn't visit, then I would end our relationship. After talking to his mother, he visited me. He made sure to tell me that his mom had made him come.

Not long after that, I decided I no longer wanted to be in a relationship with him. I began the tedious process of ending our relationship. It took a few tries, but I finally succeeded.

When I didn't have a boyfriend, Ben and I would sometimes go roller skating. One Friday evening, Ben said he had found someone interested in dating me. We were to meet him at 7:00. He said the guy was cool and thought I'd like him. Ben told the guy that I'd go on a date with him.

When we arrived at the parking lot, I felt nervous. I wasn't expecting a long-haired hippie. His car was an old, stretched vehicle. He came over to talk to us and seemed friendly enough. Ben urged me to go and have a good time. I was hesitant, but I got into his spooky car, and we drove off. The guy told me he was taking me to a party.

When we entered the party, about 30 people were sitting in a circle, smoking marijuana. He brought me over to join them. As he passed the puffer to me, I said I wasn't interested. He looked surprised and said Ben told him I do this stuff. He also mentioned that Ben had traded a date with me to get marijuana from him. I felt uncomfortable there, so I told the guy I wanted to leave. I asked him to drive me home, and he did. Later, I found out that this guy was a well-known drug dealer in the area. I can't even remember his name because I was so overwhelmed with fear and shock that Ben traded me for drugs.

I feel shocked at how brazen some boys and men can be. I had another horrible experience around Christmas that year when I went to babysit Eric and Donna's kids. They lived far out in the country on a farm. They had five children. I babysat for them once every couple of months. I bought small Christmas gifts for all the kids I regularly watched, and I brought these kids their presents that night.

When the parents returned from their outing, Eric drove me home. All the families picked me up and dropped me off because I didn't have a car. We were halfway to my house when Eric slowed his car to a stop. My heart started pounding with fear because this was out of the ordinary. He leaned over to kiss my cheek and said he wanted to thank me for getting his kids a Christmas present. I sat there, frozen and taken aback. Eric always seemed weird, and it was always awkward during the drive, but this felt dangerous.

Eric just sat there, not shifting the car into gear. He started asking me personal questions, trying to find out if I had a boyfriend. I told him I did. He made a weird comment about how he could treat me better. I gave a nervous laugh, and he still didn't show signs of driving. He sat there for what felt like 10 minutes. I was in full panic mode, not knowing what he was planning to do next. Was he ever going to put that car into drive? He was being creepy, and I felt scared.

Eric was waiting for me to show interest, and when I didn't, he apologized and finally shifted the car into gear. I felt relieved. I've never been happier to see that old farmhouse as he pulled into my driveway. Eric apologized for the rest of the drive. He knew he had crossed a huge red line and wanted to make sure he didn't lose his babysitter in the future. I got out of his car fast and never babysat for that *snake* again.

I was almost 17 years old when another fuddy-duddy boyfriend entered my life. One Friday night, I went out with Jolene and her new boyfriend, Ed. Her boyfriend brought his friend Ray along. Ray attended a Calvinist church in Canada. We hit it off and stayed in touch through phone calls and letters. After months of this long-distance relationship, I visited him. I had saved enough babysitting money to buy a plane ticket. I needed Mom's permission, but that wasn't difficult since the boy attended one of her churches. When I arrived at the airport, his mom and sister, Andrea, picked me up.

It was strange that he didn't take time off work to pick me up. It felt odd being picked up by strangers. Ray's mom and Andrea were nice, which made things easier for me. They got me settled into Andrea's room. We visited and prepared dinner while waiting for Ray to come home from work. After dinner, Ray took me downstairs to hang out in his room. I felt shocked when I saw that, near the ceiling, he had built a small wooden ledge bordering his entire room. On the ledge were 100 coffee cups with pictures of naked women on them.

My face showed my shock and disappointment. I let Ray know I wasn't happy about this kind of thing. He said his mom told him I wouldn't feel happy about it. I wish he had shared this side of himself with me before I flew to Canada. Why was his mother allowing him to keep all those coffee cups in her house? Instead of enjoying a nice vacation, it was ruined from the start as I realized this guy was just another *snake*. He would not cut the mustard for me.

After getting back home, I didn't end the relationship right away. I wasn't sure how to handle it. I had lost interest in Ray because of his cups. Whenever we talked on the phone, which was often late at night, I fell asleep on him. After a month, I broke up with him, as those coffee cups had left an unremovable scar in my brain. It's too bad because he was quite attractive. What a waste of looks to have such a filthy-minded, perverted heart.

~ Hog Wild ~

Dad drove us all to church twice every Sunday. We all crammed into our old family station wagon. During the ride, there was much fighting, elbowing, and snide, angry words. That 15-minute drive each way felt endlessly long. Nobody liked each other much. Sitting so close was like packing chickens with an egg intolerance into a vehicle and sending them to church.

On Thursday evenings, Dad drove us to catechism classes. Mom stayed home with the younger kids. Dad was a maniac driver. He did pretty well on Sundays when Mom was with us because he didn't want her yelling at him. Thursdays were a whole different story. Without Mom in the car, he went *hog wild.* The boys egged him on with their rebellious fighting. With each new stressor, he lost his temper, and his blood pressure went through the roof.

Dad cursed and yelled the entire way. Many times, he threatened to drive the wagon into the ditch and kill us all. Sometimes he swerved, making the wagon go off the edge of the road. He wanted to kill everyone, including himself, to escape it all. He was also living in hell, although it was a hell he had created.

We experienced many traumatic near-death incidents. I got carsick, especially with Dad swerving all over the place. I felt nauseous and dizzy. All I could do was sit still with my eyes closed as I avoided the elbows and kept myself from throwing up.

Each morning as I got out of bed, everything went black. I felt blind and dizzy as I made my way downstairs. I learned to navigate the steps carefully. I could see again by the time I finished going to the bathroom. I almost fell down the stairs several times, but luckily, I caught myself.

The school bus wasn't a bright yellow vehicle of childhood joy. I put my head down on the seat in front of me to avoid getting sick. It helped somewhat, but the bus was bumpy. The driver always took sharp turns. The gravel roads kicked up lots of dust that entered the inside of the bus, making me feel even worse.

I went to school every day with my head spinning. I felt better after lunch. A few hours later, I was back on the bus headed home. I tried to sleep during the ride to avoid getting sick. I sat as far to the front as possible so I could see out the windshield. It was quieter there, too. I never enjoyed sitting at the back. I didn't enjoy being near Kristi. She was a few years older than I. She was bossy and loud. In the winter, she wore a long wool coat with a matching belt tied around her waist.

One day, to find an open seat, I had to sit near the back. My sister Jolene had an open spot beside her. I sat down, knowing trouble was brewing. It wasn't long before Jolene told Kristi to sit down and shut up. Kristi, as angry as a badger, stood taller than ever and ripped her long wool belt out of its loops. She meant to take her fury out on Jolene, but since I was sitting closest, I ended up taking the brunt of her wrath.

She snapped her belt as if she were a professional belt snapper. The belt struck my face and hit my eyes, causing a sharp sting. One of my eyes couldn't even open after the long ride home. The string of nasty, *pigsty* words she spat out reminded me of my dad. She was a *muddy pig* wearing *muddy boots.*

From that day on, I sat at the front of the bus, even if I had to sit next to a boy. The mean, naughty bullies at the back were not my cup of tea. If there were no open seats, I squeezed in, sitting at the edge with my feet in the aisle. I'd do anything to avoid more abuse, besides what I already had on my plate at home.

Kristi's boyfriend, Todd, also a few years older, was also a threat I had to sidestep at school. Once, I left class to use the restroom. I was the only one in the hallway except for Todd. I stopped at the water fountain to get a drink. Todd came up behind me and put his hand on my breast. I was so startled! I had never spoken to him before. Feeling violated, I moved away from him as fast as I could and went back to class. I felt terrified that Kristi would find out and retaliate. I didn't want any more of her belt in my eyes.

The bus was not a safe place. We had a terrible bus accident when I was in third grade. It was our first year attending private school. Some guy, going *hog wild,* ran the stop sign and hit our bus. The driver always drove too fast, so he couldn't avoid the crash. The bus spiraled out of control. As it went into the ditch, the back of the bus shot straight up into the air. Then it slammed back down to a stop. Everyone flew to the front. The driver went through the windshield. I was in the front seat, so I was at the bottom of the pile. Everyone was screaming like stuck *hogs.*

Thankfully, I had landed behind the gear shifter. It protected me from everyone smashing into me. I walked away with only bruises. Susan wasn't so lucky. She landed in the stairwell with a bunch of kids piled on top of her. She ended up with a broken leg. Nathan, a boy in Harlan's class, had both of his legs broken from being in the same stairwell pile. We were all fortunate that three broken legs were the worst injuries.

A couple of years later, Jolene, Susan, Harlen, and Ben were horsing around outside on some tall, round hay bales. They were fighting. Susan was one year younger than Jolene. Jolene was a bully and had given Susan the nickname "Gug." She couldn't call Susan "ugly," so she called her Gug because it rhymed with "ug." Susan retaliated by calling Jolene, "Jo-Bean."

That day, Harlan called Susan "Gug." Susan hated being called that, especially by her younger brother. Susan pushed Harlan off the hay bales. Harlan was unhurt, but Jolene was furious with Susan for pushing Harlan. He was her ally. She was determined to make Susan pay. Jolene kicked Susan hard in the leg, and once again, broke her leg.

After breaking her leg for the second time, Susan started threatening to hit people with her crutches if they were unkind to her. Surprisingly, they backed off after she smacked them a few times.

I didn't get sick often. Being down and out meant I couldn't protect myself. When I got sick, I had to lie on the couch. It was too cold upstairs, and if I had to throw up, it was best to be near the toilet.

Harlan and Ben didn't care if someone was sick. They always yelled and fought. One time, as I lay there sick, Harlan ran and jumped on me on purpose. I told him to stop, but he backed up, ran, and did it again! I gave a frustrated sound and weakly yelled to Mom that Harlan was jumping on me. She hollered at him to knock it off. Those boys never listened! Lo and behold, wouldn't you know, he jumped on me again! A third time, and his knees jammed right into my ribs. He had now intensified his hurt on me. I released a loud, agonizing scream. It was the loudest, most prolonged scream of distress anyone in that house had ever heard. It was worse than the shrill shrieking of fifty stuck *hogs.*

I screamed over and over, only pausing to breathe. Being sick, screaming was the only way I could protect myself from abuse. I was so tired of everyone being cruel. They wouldn't even stop when I was sick. For miles, people could hear the pain in my heart as I released years of suffering from my chest. Anyone who heard me knew this was serious. They knew this scream wouldn't stop until actual help arrived. It was a scream of my being hurt and abused beyond my limits.

It worked! Mom finally paid attention. She made the boys leave me alone. If I hadn't gotten the help I needed, I would have spiraled into a complete emotional, mental, and physical shutdown without a word or sound.

That blood-curdling scream gave me strength. Nobody wanted to hear that scream of death again. Harlan and Ben backed off and stopped hurting me physically after that day. They always wrestled, trying to overpower each other. They also felt the need to overpower me. Sitting on me, they held me down and tickled me. I fought back, but they were much stronger than I was. I learned to shut my body off from feeling, mentally leaving my body, so that I could escape the torment of tickling. It took all the fun out of it for them, and they left me alone. They knew they could no longer torment me with their tickling.

When I was 13, I bought a diary with my babysitting money. It had a small key to lock it, so I believed I'd have some privacy with my writings. I kept it on my bookshelf in my room. The boys snuck into my room and read it. They exposed all my private thoughts, including my crushes.

I got my learner's permit when I was 14, and I was learning how to drive on the highway. A few years earlier, I had learned to drive the tractor. I also drove Dad's old green stick-shift truck a few times. Jesse wanted to learn how to drive a stick shift. One day, our parents went into town, and I got a *wild hair* to teach Jesse the stick. We jumped into Dad's truck, and I took Jesse, Pete, and Alex out into the cornfield.

The neighbor had harvested his field. It was the safest place so that Jesse wouldn't run into anything on the farm. Jesse was doing great with his driving. He was keeping the wheels right between the cornrows. He stalled out a lot, but I did too when I was first learning. We were having a great time and going *hog wild.* We lost track of time.

Suddenly, Pete started yelling that he saw Dad coming toward us in the station wagon! We stopped dead in our tracks! We looked hard, and sure enough, we saw that huge wagon coming fast across the field, heading straight toward us. Dad was speeding. It was bouncing up and down as he hit all the cornrows. It was clear he was furious. A massive cloud of dust was billowing up behind him.

We knew we were in serious trouble, and we feared for our lives. We were in the back corner of the field and knew that to have any chance of living, we had to outrun him. Jesse and I quickly swapped seats. I took off and sped down the cornrows as fast as I could. As we raced back to the farm, we bounced all over the place. Our butts were lifting off the seats, and our heads were banging against the ceiling.

Jesse, Pete, and Alex kept looking back as Dad chased us down. The only words I heard were, "Go! Go! Go!" and "Faster! Faster! Faster!" I shouted for them to be ready to jump out of the truck as soon as I parked it. We beat Dad back and scattered to different locations. My heart pounded for hours.

Dad never saw who was in his truck. None of us ever told him. We pretended we didn't know what he was talking about when he came huffing and puffing into the house. He demanded to know who was driving his truck. I calmly said I didn't know. I opened the stairway door and went up to my room. It was a fun little adventure while it lasted, but as with everything else, nothing fun ever lasted long.

~ String Beans ~

Every summer, we planted three enormous gardens with many rows of *string beans.* We girls went out several times a week to pick the ripe beans. We used gallon buckets to collect them. Then we snapped the ends off and snapped the beans in half. If the beans were long and skinny, we snapped them into three pieces. It was a tedious task. We filled quart jars with all the beans and then processed them in the pressure canner to seal the jars for storage.

One day, while we were snapping beans, Jolene pointed to a long, *skinny bean* and gave me my new nickname. She began calling me "String Bean." Every time, she used a tone that sounded negative and disrespectful. It made my skin crawl and my blood boil.

Jerry started the habit of giving everyone mean, rhyming nicknames. Once someone received their nickname, the other kids started using it too. Everyone laughed when someone used the hurtful nickname.

Peggy's nickname was "Boardy." She was a strong-willed, headstrong child. Jerry said her head was as hard as a board. She was stubborn, bossy, impatient, argumentative, and didn't care what anyone thought of her. She had many intense, angry outbursts.

I had to figure out how to get Jolene to stop calling me *String Bean.* After thinking about it, I told her I enjoyed being skinny and asked if she felt jealous. It backfired. Jolene went for the throat. I avoided having any weaknesses that she could use against me, but I had one. I wet the bed. To keep her name-calling consistent with rhyme, she began calling me "Twis" because it rhymed with wetting the bed.

Jolene was a complete jerk. I had to break. She won. I thought I could stand up to her. However, the risk of her calling me Twis at school or on the bus was high. She would have said it in front of visiting aunts and uncles. It would have caused me extreme embarrassment because she also would have revealed why she called me that name.

Luckily, some of my other siblings also wet the bed. When they started calling me Twis, I called them out on it. I asked if I should start calling them Twis as well. They saw my point, and they stopped calling me names altogether. They realized that the hurtfulness was reaching a deep personal level that could also expose them.

Jolene was mean. She had learned a lot from all the mean adults in our house. She became rebellious and bossy. Jolene thought she had to be an abuser to escape abuse. Once, Mom went into town. To punish Pete, Jolene put him in the dryer and turned it on. I screamed at her to stop and rushed to get Pete out of the dryer. She then locked us outside.

When we switched to the church's private school, Mom held Jolene back a grade because the new school only went to eighth grade. She had to retake eighth grade and was in Susan's class. They hated being in the same class. The kids in their class teased Jolene. Barb was very mean and snotty to her. She was the ringleader who teased Jolene. She teased her about being held back. On many days, Jolene came home from school crying because of the nasty remarks Barb made to her. She went straight to her room to mourn her broken heart. She was getting a taste of her own medicine.

Jolene realized she preferred being friends with boys. This made Barb jealous and even more abusive toward her. Wanting the boys for herself, Barb made Jolene's life miserable. She looked down on her and made snide and hurtful remarks.

Jolene rebelled against all of Mom's house rules. She started wearing jeans on her dates, bought makeup, and wore it openly. Mom couldn't control her and often yelled at her, trying to make her listen. One day, Jolene was leaving the house in a pair of tight jeans. Mom, in a fit of anger, shouted out to her, "Those jeans look horrible on you." Mom's words made Jolene's blood boil. In her mind, Mom had just called her fat. If Mom were going to call her fat, then she would show her! She would punish her!

Jolene stopped eating. Whenever she ate, she threw it up. Mom became worried as Jolene continued to refuse to eat. The more Mom tried to make her eat, the more Jolene wouldn't. Jolene became very thin and malnourished.

Mom asked the doctor what to do. He instructed her to bring Jolene to the hospital. Mom checked Jolene out of her class and admitted her to the hospital. Jolene was furious that Mom was making her go. Nobody was going to control her! Ever!

The hospital could not help Jolene recover. She refused help and wanted to die. During her group sessions, the other teens talked about how they were harming themselves. Jolene learned many new ways to further her death wish.

Jolene started drinking lots of ice water to suppress her appetite. I found many boxes of laxatives hidden in the back of her closet. All of them were empty. She had learned these new tricks at the hospital. Jolene was trying to become as thin as possible. Her entire focus was on food and how to avoid it. Watching her waste away into nothingness was frightening. The sad irony is — she turned into the *String Bean.*

She internalized all her anger. The only thing she could control was food. She wanted to punish Mom, Dad, and the girls in her class. She believed that if she were no longer here, they'd all regret it. The pain in her heart was great. Her mother had told her she was fat. Come what may, she was going to make Mom pay. When she was gone, they'd be sorry then.

I got a much-needed break from her being mean to me, but the damage had already been done. Jolene had beaten me down, and my heart now carried many cuts, stabs, and wounds. I felt sad. There was no love in our home. There was no escape, and no help was coming. A few years after Jolene became anorexic and bulimic, I followed the same path.

After many years of calling the police for help, social services started visiting our farm. When I overheard two social service workers talking with Mom, I felt a flicker of hope that they might help. No one had helped before, but these women sounded determined. They recommended that we all talk to a therapist. My therapist suggested I go to the hospital. Once there, I was required to join group workshops. They handed out papers teaching me how to handle stress and control my emotions.

They held a session on assertiveness. I felt encouraged that there might be something to help me stand up for myself. They explained that I can't control other people's behavior. I had to focus only on my behavior and words. They taught me to focus on who I want to be. They emphasized that it is my behavior that defines me. I learned to say, "I feel hurt" instead of "You hurt me." I also learned that the word "you" is accusatory, while "I" emphasizes what I can control. They taught me that it was essential to love myself.

I felt hopeful when I got back home from the hospital. Nobody checked on me to see if I was okay. They swept it all under the rug as if it had never happened. Sarah, a girl in my class, gave me a get-well card from her family. I was thankful for her kindness, but I felt embarrassed that everyone knew about my business. It didn't surprise me, though, since talking behind other people's backs was their specialty. They didn't offer any real comfort or help.

My sister, Danielle, added insult to injury. She told me she used to look up to me, but now she disrespects me. I needed love and support from her, but she offered judgment and condemnation. I was all alone and had no one to comfort me. Everything happening around me felt terrible. There had to be a better way.

I still struggled with an eating disorder, but I had gained some tools to practice assertiveness. My siblings teased me when I started using "I feel" statements. The hospital taught me that I could use the "I feel" and "I felt" statements in a calm tone of voice and then simply walk away. They said that to be the opposite of who they are, I needed to act and speak in a way that was opposite of how they acted and spoke. That made sense to me. It actually made complete sense.

I was thankful that my therapist had advised me to go to the hospital. The eating disorder didn't disappear overnight, but it put me on a path to stand up for myself. They showed me how to express my hurt and pain in a healthy, assertive way.

After receiving a little help, I felt a bit stronger. I met some kind people who seemed to care, and also met some other kids who lived in abusive homes. I no longer felt so alone. There were others. Sadly, there were many others.

~ Pots and Kettles ~

When Jolene was 17, she started working at a pizza restaurant, where she met Rick. He was a tall, lanky boy with many nervous tics and allergies. They started dating. After introducing him to our family, he sometimes came over to see her and played board games with us. After a few months, Jolene broke up with him because she couldn't handle his allergies.

Susan felt sorry for Rick and liked him enough to date him. She became pregnant. She and Rick had committed the unforgivable sin. Mom was beside herself with grief that her daughter had gotten pregnant before marriage. Her embarrassment and shame were visible. Her face became twisted in torment. The entire church would talk about this. It would be the talk of the town.

Susan and Rick got married. Rick was unkind to their little boy, so Mom started talking about him behind his back. Naturally, the boys took this as their cue to be cruel to him as well. They began imitating his nervous tics and sniffing. They became so hurtful toward Rick that he and Susan stopped visiting.

Mom's church taught that premarital intimacy was a sin. If someone became pregnant before marriage, church leaders shamed the couple by making them stand in front of the congregation to confess their guilt and shame.

They can't have a church wedding or become members until they confess. After their public shaming, the preacher gives a sermon to the teenagers. He emphasizes how much this sin displeases God and instills fear in them to discourage them from committing it.

Parents also attempt to prevent their teenagers from engaging in intimate relationships. They often use derogatory, hateful slurs toward the unborn baby. They call it an illegitimate or bastard baby.

Teenagers receive complete brainwashing that premarital intimacy is dirty, shameful, and sinful. Church leaders know that teenagers become curious about intimacy. However, they believe God's perfect plan for puberty and intimacy needs some adjustment. They teach that God requires that we suppress all those wild, intense urges until marriage.

Teenagers are told that God becomes angry if they engage in premarital intimacy. Then, if they became pregnant, they had to beg for His forgiveness and express their sorrow for their "sin." Everyone wants to witness these "sinful" couples humiliated, so there is a large crowd at church on these Sunday evenings.

The only time people are required to make a public confession is when someone gets pregnant. The gossipers and abusers never have to confess their sins and shame publicly.

These church folks are a bunch of *pots calling the kettle black*. Not one of them dares to admit that they also committed this "unforgivable sin" of premarital intimacy. They can't let anyone know about their teenage acts of intimacy. If their secret got out, they'd become the subjects of gossip and backbiting. They know that the judgment and criticism from others would be harsh. They could never go out in public again without feeling ashamed.

Everyone keeps this huge secret deep in their hearts. The only way to keep their teenage intimacy hidden is to be cruel to those who become pregnant before marriage. If they criticize the pregnant couple, no one will ever suspect that they also had been intimate during their teenage years.

If the church leaders ever found out, they would be required to stand in church and confess their guilt and shame. Their secret must remain with them for the rest of their lives! The risk is too great.

They never allow their feelings of guilt to surface. Whenever they catch a brief glimpse, they quickly look away. It makes them feel sad, depressed, and terrified. It is best to keep those feelings suppressed and never let them resurface again. Instead, they focus on other people's mistakes while hiding their own mistakes under the rug.

Everyone feels afraid of hell. The leaders tell them they are in a constant state of sin and that their sins keep piling up. They beg God daily to forgive their enormous pile of sins. The preacher doesn't teach them how to love our Heavenly Father, themselves, and others. They also don't teach them the importance of taking personal responsibility, apologizing, and asking forgiveness from others when they have hurt them.

No, they don't want to teach this simple message of love, apology, and forgiveness. This doesn't instill fear in the people. Keeping people afraid means fuller *money pots.* It's a way for them to maintain power. If they didn't instill fear, they'd lose their authority as the "holy men of God."

It's unusual for these shepherds to relinquish their power over the people. They have to if they get caught having an affair or abusing a child. However, even then, they say whatever it takes to keep their positions. The parishioners don't believe the allegations against their "holy man" because their reverence for him is very high. They either blame the victim or dismiss the accusations as false.

These same church leaders never mention that using degrading slurs toward babies and children should never be done. They don't preach sermons about how gossip, backbiting, judging, and criticizing are hurtful. The shepherd doesn't teach the people to love and forgive themselves.

Looking back, I realize that the person who feels the most guilt and shame about their mistakes often becomes the most judgmental and critical toward others making similar mistakes. The more they try to hide their guilt, the louder they criticize others.

It was a difficult and heavy spiritual path that we traveled. We believed we were terrible sinners and unworthy of God's love. Most spend their entire lives in fear, guilt, and shame. They don't love themselves and don't forgive themselves for their mistakes.

It's shocking how these preachers keep everyone terrified that God will condemn them to hell. It definitely works. There's no doubt about that! Everyone feels scared, so they keep going back and sit in those pews week after week, after fearful week.

We were told that God speaks directly through the preacher. We feared leaving our spot in church empty because they said that missing church was slapping God in the face. The reverend said God will throw us into an unquenchable, burning fire forever. Hopefully, when these preachers pass away, they think ahead and have some *pots and kettles* placed in their coffins. No stove necessary!

~ Half Baked Eggs ~

One day, when I was 16, Dad was being cruel to one of my brothers. As I walked past the garage, I told him to knock it off and leave them alone. He flew into a rage. He grabbed a nearby screwdriver, held it up high, and charged at me, threatening to run me through with it. I rushed into the house and attempted to lock him outside, but he was too fast and too strong. He barged through the door. There was nobody to protect me — no one to help.

As I ran through the porch, Dad was right on my heels, and I barely made it to the kitchen doorway. I knew I had to fight back or die. Spinning around, I screamed at him to stop! I told him I was sick and tired of him hurting everyone and asked him who he thought he was. He had his screwdriver inches from my stomach. I stayed firm in my resolve to end his terror and tried to grab the screwdriver from him. When my attempt failed, I pushed him. He stumbled back, giving me enough time to shout for him to leave me alone. Then I rushed to the bathroom and locked the door.

He chased after me. I was shaking in my boots. I feared he would break down the door. He spat out his final string of curse words and insults, threatened to kill me in the middle of the night, and then everything went eerily quiet. I didn't dare leave the bathroom for fear that he was waiting outside the door. I heard no sound to suggest he had left the house or moved away from the bathroom door.

I spent an hour in the bathroom. When Mom got home from her bus route, I slowly opened the door. I knew he wouldn't remain there when he heard Mom arrive. I went straight to her bus and told her what had happened. In a stern voice, I warned her that something had to be done fast, or we'd all end up dead.

In the coming days, Mom talked to the elders of her church. After weeks of deliberation, they said she could get a legal separation from Dad. They didn't allow her a divorce. Only *half* of a divorce. My mom hired a lawyer, filed for separation, and had the sheriff come to escort Dad off the farm.

Our fear of death didn't stop. Often, things went missing. He was coming in the middle of the night. Guns went missing, and we kept living in fear of him shooting us dead. Mom changed the locks, but we knew that if Dad wanted in, nothing could stop him.

Dad moved into a small house in town. He picked up the younger kids every other Saturday. He took them fishing or to the park. I didn't go with him because I didn't like him. I never wanted to see him again. He made the kids feel sorry for him and persuaded them to ask Mom to let him come back. She said no.

Dad, feeling lonely, visited Anna, hoping to get her sympathy. While he was there, she had to leave the room. When she returned, she caught him digging through her kitchen drawers. She had intense flashbacks of him with knives and felt an eerie suspicion that he was looking to steal something. Anna told him that if he was going to dig through her belongings, he needed to leave. She knew he had been sneaking into our house to take guns. After she moved out, she visited his siblings and discovered he had stolen their guns when they were younger. She didn't trust him, so she got him out of her house quickly.

Over the years, the police advised Dad to check himself into a mental health hospital, which he did twice. At the hospital, they diagnosed schizophrenia and high blood pressure. They prescribed medication for both conditions. However, nothing changed at home. Sometimes he took his medicine, but most of the time he didn't. After he returned home, things remained calm for a few days. That was just the calm before the storm. Something always made him fly off the handle. He went back to grabbing his prized weapons.

Six years after my parents' legal separation, after I married and had children of my own, I felt compelled to visit Dad. The only fond memory I had of him was when he played his accordion. I may have wanted to hear him play it one last time. If Mom had allowed him to play his accordion as often as he wanted, he might have been a somewhat different dad. We might not have hated him as much if he had given us musical joy. Also, I was searching for answers, so I called him up and arranged a visit.

The visit went well. Dad's house was small. It had one tiny bedroom and a combined living room and kitchen area. He didn't look well. I thought he appeared frail, so I didn't feel threatened. He looked as if he were on his last leg in life. I didn't ask the questions I wanted to, and I didn't get the answers I was hoping for. I asked him to play his accordion. He had a hard time lifting that heavy thing onto his shoulders. He played only one song before he had to put it away.

I didn't stay long. There was an unpleasant smell in Dad's house. It was also hot because he had no air conditioning. I needed to see if he was any different. He seemed pretty tame, but that was probably because of his health. I left his house feeling sad. I knew I'd never get the answers to why he was the way he was. Tears of loss and pain flowed freely down my face the entire way home.

A year later, when I was 23, Mom received a phone call from Dad's friend, Marjorie. They had met at the veterans' hospital and kept in touch. Marjorie lived quite far away, but they talked on the phone often to keep each other company. She asked Mom to check on Dad because she had been trying to call him for a few days. He wasn't answering, which she said was unusual.

Mom checked on him but didn't knock on the door. She knew he had died when she approached. The smell coming from his house was unmistakably that of death. She called the emergency services, who responded and found him. He had been lying dead in that small house for three days. He suffered a heart attack and could not get to the phone. At the funeral home, they told us he was not presentable and recommended that no one view the body. They said it had to be a closed casket. Jerry was the only one who saw Dad and said his goodbyes. Dad was almost 65 years old.

Dad's death was a relief for me because I no longer had to live in fear of him. He couldn't hurt any of us physically anymore. All the pain and suffering he inflicted were enough to last a thousand lifetimes. The grief and loss of what should have been will hang over our heads for the rest of our lives.

The old chicken house burned down in an electrical fire. Many chickens had died by the time the fire department arrived. Most of the eggs were *half-baked.* Inside the walls were hundreds of smashed beer cans. Dad and the boys had stuffed them there over the years to hide them from Mom.

The aftereffects of enduring severe abuse and trauma in childhood differ from one child to another. Some kids, to hide the deep scars on their hearts, became calloused and adopted a generalized "I don't care" attitude to protect themselves from further pain. If we push people away, then they can't hurt us. Some developed a codependent relationship with Mom, always attempting to please her and striving to be the child that "mother loves best."

Some became mean and rude. Others became alcoholics, developed eating disorders, or became gossiping backbiters. Some continued in the vicious cycle of physical and verbal abuse within their families. They yelled, cursed, and acted angry at their children. Others choose to remain in the same extreme religion, and they pass the same religious abuse down to their children. They learned from the best.

It's upsetting to realize how many homes suffer severe abuse. Most of my brothers and sisters will spend their lives as scrambled eggs. Some have received just enough help to survive and get by. Others pretend it wasn't so bad as they continue the same behavior. A couple of lucky ones realized that, with all the curveballs, it was crucial to get a strong bat. They have found peace, joy, love, and happiness — becoming sunny-side up.

~ Fox in the Henhouse ~

When I was almost 18, I started working at a grocery store in a nearby town. There, I met Dale. He was married when I met him. He used pity tricks on me, claiming his wife was cheating on him. Dale said that he had stopped doing drugs, but she wouldn't stop. I was a naive young girl from a sheltered and severely abusive home. I felt sorry for him. He was ten years older than I was, and by playing his pity card, he seduced me into believing his lies. We began seeing each other, and each time he continued with his story of being a wounded, betrayed husband.

I don't remember how Mom found out I was seeing this guy, but she did. She called my school principal, Dale's dad, and the preacher. If Mom had left well enough alone, I would have eventually dumped him, and most likely sooner rather than later. However, she didn't, and it ultimately forced me to run away with him to escape the extreme embarrassment she was causing me.

I was in a tough spot because she had called in the troops to help her remove him from my life. I couldn't go back to school because the principal would call me into his office, and I didn't want to discuss my personal life with him. Going to work would be awkward. Dale's dad owned the grocery store, and now he knew it too. I didn't want to face him either. The way gossip spread in my area was remarkable. Within a day, everyone would have heard the big news. As a result, I wouldn't be able to show my face at church or anywhere else without people whispering and gossiping as I passed by. Thanks a lot, Mom!

To avoid all the troops Mom had called in, I ran away with Dale to get out of the wood chipper she had put me in. Once three hours away, I felt like I could breathe. Dale got a divorce, and after a few months, I became pregnant! Shoot a pickle! Now I had to cover up this "unforgivable sin." I quickly married him to hide the pregnancy. I thought I could say the baby was premature and had come early.

It didn't take long for Dale to show his true nature. He was going to strip clubs and hanging out with drug users. He also had anger issues, to the point where he got mad at me for eating French fries out of the fast food bag before we returned home. One time, the druggie in the apartment next door had friends over. They had a baby who wouldn't stop screaming. I was pregnant with Heather, and I was worried that they were neglecting their baby. Dale went over and knocked on his door. He told him to take care of the crying baby. The neighbor's friend came out and punched Dale, breaking his nose.

I had never driven in a big city before, and I totaled our car. I made a last-second swerve to catch the exit off the interstate. The car spun out of control and rolled over into the ditch. I later found out that the car's tires were bald. Luckily, we weren't hurt.

Dale worked at a car dealership and secretly took a car home. He claimed it was a hush-hush deal, and a manager let him use it as his dealer car. When I learned Dale had taken the car without permission, I became worried. I insisted we get rid of it. Dale was a sneaky, shady character — always lying and feeling entitled to whatever he wanted.

A year later, we moved to Wyoming. Dale said he got a job through a newspaper ad managing an apartment complex. Shockingly, when we arrived, Dale didn't have a job lined up as an apartment manager. I found a job at a restaurant in town, and Dale found work at a rock quarry.

One morning, when I was heading out to work, I couldn't find our car. I called the restaurant to let them know I'd be late because I had to walk. I explained that our car was missing. Dale told me later that the car company repossessed it because he wasn't making the payments. He thought that if he moved far away, he could avoid paying for it. He believed they wouldn't find us in Wyoming.

Six months after we moved, his two sisters came to visit. We were playing cards with the cook, who worked at the same restaurant. We were only using pennies, nickels, and dimes, but thinking that I had a great hand, I bet him $10, and of course, I lost it. Dale went ballistic in front of his sisters. He was shouting at me and cursing me out. I felt utterly humiliated. He was no better than my dad with his rage behavior.

I knew we couldn't afford to bet money like that. It wasn't something I had ever done before. We could barely afford to buy diapers. Many times, we had to use cloth diapers because we didn't have any money. He was showing off to his sisters how big and tough he was.

He got physical and hit me once. I went to the neighbors to call the pastor of the church we were attending. He never did it again. He knew I'd tell someone important if he hit me. For many years, I suffered from situational depression. I was stuck with an abusive man. I had gotten myself into the same frying pan that many women before me had also gotten themselves into.

Four years after running away, we moved back to be near Mom. I thought I was homesick. However, I didn't realize it, but it was codependency pulling me back to her. I had also become brainwashed with her church's doctrine, so I wanted to return to attend her "God's only truth" church.

~ Fowl Play ~

After moving and settling in, I went to the post office to get a P.O. box for our mail. While I was there, I ran into Amy — the girl I had been friends with in third grade — the girl who had accused me of stealing her wallet and had turned the entire class against me for an entire year. I hadn't seen her in years. After sixth grade, her parents took her out of the private school and re-enrolled her in public school. She seemed excited to see me. Since we lived only two blocks apart, she asked if we could hang out sometime. I said yes — that would be great! Since she was an adult, married, and had kids, I thought our girls could *play* together.

After we started hanging out, her 5-year-old daughter, Kim, randomly showed up at my house to *play* with my kids. Kim was a mean little girl. She eerily reminded me of Amy when she was younger and how she had treated me back in grade school. Kim demanded to have whatever toy she wanted and was mean to my girls if they didn't give it to her. I had to send her home frequently because of her misbehavior.

When my daughter Hannah turned 5, I threw a birthday party for her. I asked Amy if she could drive some kids in her car to the bowling alley. My vehicle wouldn't fit all of them. She agreed. On the afternoon of Hannah's party, before any kids arrived, a lady from Social Services showed up at my door. She told me she had received a call from someone concerned that my children were eating cat poop.

My jaw hit the floor. What in the tarnation! Who could have done such a thing?

I showed the lady around my home. I felt devastated. She asked the girls if it was true. They told her it wasn't. The lady apologized for the inconvenience. She said she could see that the allegations were false. After she left, I was furious. I knew who had done this terrible thing. The only people in my life cruel enough to do such a horrendous act were Amy and her devil child. Kim had gotten mad at one of my girls. She lied to Amy to retaliate against them. The egg doesn't fall far from the chicken.

The party! Amy, Kim, and all of Hannah's little school friends would arrive in 15 minutes. I couldn't go back on my word to Hannah. She was excited and looking forward to going bowling with her friends. To get everyone there, I needed Amy. When Amy arrived, I was ready to go, so I didn't talk to her. I just started loading everyone into her car.

While the children were bowling, I barely spoke to Amy. I deliberately kept busy helping the kids. My blood was boiling the entire time we were there. Just being near Amy made my skin crawl. I needed her to take the children back, so I couldn't say anything about what she had done to me. I had to wait until we were back home.

Once home, my gloves came off. I sent all the kids into the house to play, and I let Amy have it. I gave it to her big time. All the hurt and pain she had caused me in fourth grade rose to the surface as I walked over to her car. I didn't even ask her if she had called Social Services. I knew she was the only one capable of doing such a terrible act.

As I approached Amy, I told her that the social services lady had come earlier, and she informed me she had received a complaint about the kids eating cat poop. Amy's face turned white as a ghost. That was my confirmation that I could proceed with giving her a royal butt-chewing. I thought my anger was at its highest level before I started speaking to her, but when her face went pale, my blood boiled, and I began shouting at her. I asked her how she could do such a thing. She began to answer, but I cut her off. I didn't want to hear any of her excuses.

I tore into her hard, chewing her out and telling her she hadn't changed at all since her childhood cruelty, and now she has a daughter who is exactly like her. I yelled at her about how much she hurt me in fourth grade when she accused me of stealing her wallet and turned the entire class against me. My face was red as I told her I wanted nothing more to do with her. I also shouted that I didn't want her little demon child to show up at my door ever again either.

Amy was beside herself. She was visibly shaking as her chicken feet stumbled to my front door to retrieve her devil child. Her terror was so great that she literally forgot to take her car. She was dragging her demonic child as she ran away from my house. I yelled at her again to never come back, and that I never wanted to see her face ever again. I'm sure that, as I've never forgotten this incident, the memory is forever scarred in her brain as well.

I don't normally use *fowl* language, but I definitely used some toward Amy that day. I didn't want any more of her *fowl play.* She had taught her little birdie to be just like her. I could not allow this, for myself or my children. She can take her beak stabbing elsewhere. I refused to let her peck at me any longer. Her little chick was not going to chirp at my baby duckies.

Amy is a broken toaster who will always give burnt toast. I don't like burnt toast. It tastes nasty! You can try scraping off the burnt parts, but it never tastes good, no matter how much butter or honey you put on it.

~ Cracked Eggs ~

For Dale and me to become members of Mom's church, we had to attend its faith classes every Friday night. We also had to stand in front of the entire congregation, along with the others who had gotten pregnant before marriage, to make a public confession of our guilt and shame.

After we jumped through all their hoops, the consistory of elders and deacons then voted and decided we could not join their church. They claimed they saw me as being in a constant state of adultery, married to a married man. They didn't recognize his divorce as biblically valid, so they considered him still married to his first wife. *What on earth were these guys smoking?*

They said that anyone who is in a continuous state of sin isn't eligible to become a member. Many of them believe that only members of their church can enter heaven — but only if God has predestined them to go there. Essentially, because they denied us membership, they were also denying us entry into heaven. They implied in their vote that our destiny was hell.

I felt insulted and shocked that these men had rejected us. I thought it was wrong of them to deny us membership. Deciding never to return, we visited several other churches in the area. None of them felt right. I had been brainwashed with the predestination-only doctrine. Those other churches were teaching that everyone has free will.

One day, a woman at the Women, Infants, and Children's office gave me a recording of a television minister. She asked me to listen to it and let her know what I thought. I started listening to it, and boy oh boy, was I ever going to prove her minister wrong! He was teaching the most outlandish things. I had heard nothing like it before! I would give this woman my full review! As I replayed the recording, I used Strong's Concordance of the Bible this time. I was going to write down everything I disagreed with and tell her exactly why her minister was wrong.

Well, the exact opposite happened. I *cracked.* Surprisingly, I experienced a complete spiritual awakening. My brainwashing became nonexistent in two shakes of a lamb's tail. This television minister was correct. Now, I wanted to move closer to this church. Mom's church had just rejected me. I had been told my entire life that her church is God's only truth. Finding a church that actually taught the Bible in such depth, chapter by chapter and verse by verse, completely blew my mind. The Bible now made perfect sense to me, whereas it had never made sense before.

Because Mom's church had a no birth control rule, I had four little children, one right after the other. That didn't stop me from moving, though. I realized, without a doubt, that I did not want to live in the vulture pit with these judgmental, critical, and gossipy people. We moved 10 hours away to Minnesota, and I never looked back!

I worked hard to raise my children differently from how I had grown up. I aimed to break the vicious cycle of abuse and made a complete 180° turn compared to the abusive home I grew up in. Using positive reinforcement, I told them how smart they are and taught them to use phrases like 'I'm sorry,' 'please,' and 'thank you.' I did a good job — though not perfect by any means. It was much better than what I experienced during my traumatic childhood. Maybe I spoiled my kids too much. I probably didn't teach them properly about the birds and the bees, or how broken toasters will give them burnt toast. Working so hard growing up, I didn't want them to have to work as hard as I did, so perhaps I fell short in that area. Sometimes I might have been too strict.

They don't realize how thankful they should be to the lady who gave me those Bible teachings. It completely changed my life — and ultimately, theirs as well. I had been raising them at my mom's church! I almost led them down the same abusive religious path I had endured for many years. We dodged a huge bullet. I should send thank-you notes and flowers to those elders and deacons every day.

I was now in a safe place and no longer living near a cemetery of buzzards. However, I was married to a man who would lie, cheat, steal, go to strip clubs, and indulge in pornography. I had four small kids and a broken toaster that felt more like a fifth child to me.

Over the years, I often wished I could have divorced Dale. I had to stay with him because I couldn't support four small children on $6.00 an hour plus daycare costs. I longed for the day they graduated from high school so I could be free of this perverted liar and thief.

He often stole money from my purse, claiming that a burglar did it. Sometimes he tried to make me think I had used the money myself. It happened so often that I literally had to put a padlock on my purse to keep him out. The word 'burglar' came out of his mouth so much that I had him install a security system. It's funny that he could never get the cameras to work correctly.

He stole money from the kids' savings envelope and lied, claiming the babysitter took it. He also stole my credit cards from my purse. Since I never used them, I didn't realize they were missing until I saw he had maxed them out. He was so convincing with his lies that I believed him many times. He acted as if he didn't know what I was talking about.

Over the years, he threw pity parties and borrowed enormous sums of money from his dad, never paying him back a penny. Like a *fox in a henhouse,* he stole whatever he wanted, whenever he wanted, then lied to cover it up. I felt like I was going out of my mind. I was always on high alert, filled with anxiety, and suffering from situational depression.

One evening, I went to open the gun safe only to find that it wouldn't open. I took the keypad cover off, and lo and behold, wouldn't ya know, Dale had cut all the wires. He lied through his teeth, swearing it was a burglar and even swearing on the Bible and his dad's life that he didn't do it. I had believed him in the past. Who swears on the Bible and then lies? I didn't believe him at this point. He had cut the wires way in the back so that I couldn't reattach them.

The next day, while he was at work, I bought some wiring and connectors. Using tweezers, I connected all the wires to longer pieces, making them easier to work with. I attached and numbered each wire. Tediously, I had to wire, rewire, and test the code repeatedly to see if I could get it to open.

There were ten different wires inside, and none of them had color-coding. I had to try hundreds of wiring configurations, writing each one down as I went through them. It took me two full days, but finally, it worked. I *cracked* the safe. Of course, Dale had stolen and pawned everything, leaving the safe completely bare.

Dale was lazy and didn't want to work. He preferred to sit in front of the TV watching sports. He was a huge procrastinator. I often got upset with him to get him to do things that needed to be done. Some squirrels watch where other squirrels hide their nuts, and then they steal them. Dale was one of those squirrelly nuts. Thief was his middle name.

Because of his laziness, Dale exploited others and lived in a vicious cycle of deception. He did landscaping and told me he had finished jobs when he didn't, and vice versa. Dale did sloppy work. People couldn't get him to return to make the necessary repairs. He spent a lot of energy being *sly as a fox.* He had no clue that it would have taken much less energy to just work honestly and do things right.

Dale did some work for Ron, a builder, but he did shabby work. He didn't answer the phone when Ron called him to come back and fix his mistakes. After months of being ignored and lied to, the builder grew furious with Dale's broken promises. One day, Ron was following Dale down the road. He caught up to Dale's truck and forced him off the road to make him stop. Once stopped, Ron ran back to Dale. He yanked him out of his truck, punched him repeatedly, and broke his nose. The builder didn't stop there. He also *cracked* his head against the truck, pushed him into the door frame, and began slamming and smashing Dale with the truck door. I understand Ron's fury because if I were a guy,

I might have done the same to Dale. Nothing but lies, theft, and broken promises. Dirty ol' Dale.

One day, while doing laundry, I found a post office key at the bottom of the washing machine. I called Dale to ask him about it. He swore it wasn't his. When I continued questioning him, he then remembered picking up a key off the floor of his truck. He claimed it must belong to one of the workers. I didn't believe him and told him so. Slyly, he called me shortly afterward and had his worker tell me it was his key. The lengths he would go to cover his lies! Of course, I *cracked* the case later when I found out that Dale had a secret post office box. He used it to keep me from seeing the mail. Sometimes, I'd find a big hidden stash of lies — a bag full of mail — that he had hidden on the shelves in the garage or elsewhere, wherever he thought I wouldn't find it.

Dale lost our family home to foreclosure right under my nose. He lied and said everything was fine. In reality, it was far from fine. One day, the sheriff posted a note on our door, saying we had three days to vacate. The bank had sold our house at auction.

Thank the dear Lord above that I could find a home to move into. We had to put all our belongings into storage. Later, I discovered Dale was removing everything from storage to sell and pawn. I'm sure he planned to tell me that a burglar had broken into the storage unit and stolen everything. When he forgot his wallet at home one day, I opened it to see if he was hiding anything from me.

Shockingly, I found a pawn receipt for my wedding ring. I had stopped wearing it. I told him I'd put it on if he ever wanted to be married without all the lies and pornography. Finding this receipt made me wonder what else he might have pawned. I hoped he hadn't pawned my little three-pearl ring. I had little jewelry. Just that cute pearl ring. It was my favorite. I could never wear it because I kept bumping into things and knocking the pearls off.

When he returned home, I asked him if he would go to the storage to get my jewelry boxes. He was gone for a few hours. I'm sure he was planning what lies he would tell me. He most likely had put two and two together after accidentally leaving his wallet at home, and now I'm asking him to retrieve my jewelry. He knew he wouldn't get away with lying to me about this one.

When he returned, he told me he couldn't find the box. I knew he was lying because he had just been inside that box and pawned my wedding ring. I was at the end of my rope. It was too much, and I couldn't hold it in anymore. I needed to get this off my chest. I had been suppressing it for over 20 years. As I *cracked,* it burst out of me like a raging waterfall. Like a wounded animal caught in a trap, I let out the most terrifying scream of my life. It was a scream of bloody murder.

After everything he had already stolen from me — all his lies, losing our family home, and now him stealing and pawning everything else too — I screamed so long and hard that Dirty Dale looked at me in horror and asked, "What is wrong with you!?" I let him have it, telling him exactly what was wrong with me. He quickly left. He didn't want to hear anything I had to say. I'm not a cussing woman, but that day, I'm sure our Heavenly Father had to cover His ears.

As a child, I screamed when my brothers and sisters were mean to me. It was the only way I knew how to make them stop. However, on this day, as I *cracked,* I let out an unforgettable, ear-piercing scream. It was a scream filled with all of my built-up pain and suffering that I had endured for too long. It came from being hurt and betrayed beyond belief. That scream will haunt Dale's soul until the day he dies.

We separated at one point near the end of our marriage. One night, I told him I wanted a divorce. He stormed off. When he came back into the house, he slammed a handgun down in front of me. He told me, "You aren't worth it!" I guess he had been thinking about taking his life, but decided against it. I called the police, and they took him to jail. We separated for a few months after that.

During our separation, he approached the parents of our children's friends and told them things I said about them. Given his lies, I'm sure he also made up many false stories. He tried to turn anyone and everyone against me. Shockingly, he even went to my sister Anna to make me look like a dirty bird. He played the pity party with our daughter, Hannah, and convinced her to come live with him. If he was going out, he was going to do it with a bang.

When we first moved to Minnesota, I befriended an older woman named Janice. She was in her late fifties. We met her because our vehicle broke down right outside her home. She came out to see if we needed help. During our separation, I was giving away an old refrigerator from the garage. Janice's cousin Billy wanted it. When Billy came to pick up the fridge, we discussed what was going on with Dale. He told me that one time, when he stopped to visit Janice, and as he approached her house, Dale stormed out yelling, "The price is too high!"

Billy said that "my friend" became addicted to painkillers and that she and Dale were probably involved in some kind of drug dealing behind my back. It all made sense now. Janice had asked me multiple times to get her some cold medicine from the store. She said it had to be purchased through the pharmacist because they only allowed her to buy a certain amount each month, but she needed more. Billy told me that this cold medicine was used to make drugs. He said she was selling it to people. It also now made sense why Dale had recently started hanging out with a known drug user in town.

I thought Janice was a genuine friend. I helped her financially quite a bit. What a massive deception! They both completely fooled me. She was at the nursing home when I found this out. The next time I visited, I asked her about it. She denied it and said Billy was lying. I no longer knew what to believe. My world was so full of lies. I couldn't tell up from down anymore. I didn't go back to see her again. She died about a year later.

~ Broken Toasters ~

After we separated, whatever Dale told his dad and stepmom must have been off the wall. The next time I saw them, I went over to say hello. Wayne was cordial and returned my hug. When I reached out to hug Wanda, she literally pulled back as if I had maggots crawling all over me. I'm sure Dale played his pity-party tricks and told his parents all kinds of lies to make me look terrible and himself seem like the wounded husband. He probably told Wanda that I said I didn't like her. He was telling her the truth about that! She was a *broken toaster!* The only thing she knew how to give was burnt toast.

Dale's birth mother, Christine, died in a train-car accident when he was five. He told me he remembered people telling him that his mom had died. However, he said he felt nothing and didn't even cry about it. I always thought that was unnaturally odd. I remember Anna leaving home, and I cried my eyes out for months. She was my Nana, my mommy. I couldn't understand how he could feel nothing at all.

I walked on eggshells around Wanda. She was condescending and always looked down her nose at others. She was judgmental, critical, and degrading, always making snide comments. When Hannah was 4 years old, Wanda spanked her for not putting her pants on correctly.

Hannah felt scared around Wanda, so I had Heather accompany her on her birthday outing to help Hannah feel less afraid. Once, Hannah accidentally wet the bed during an overnight visit to their house. Wanda treated her harshly and recklessly put her in the bathtub. After several incidents, I stopped allowing the girls to visit her house.

When Dale was little, Wanda pushed his nose into his poo when he had an accident. He told me she often hit him with tennis shoes so she wouldn't leave any marks. She was mean, and because he was terrified of her, he tried to stay away from her at all costs. Dale became rebellious and lied to her to avoid getting in trouble. He spent a lot of time at his dad's grocery store. There, he could take whatever he wanted whenever he wanted to. This made him feel entitled, which later led him to believe he could do the same to anyone he pleased.

Dale's two brothers were also married, and Wanda picked on the three of us wives at every get-together. Once, I set a baby bottle on her mantel. She looked down her nose at me and scolded me for placing it on her wooden ledge. I had to stay on guard around her because she would unleash her judgment and criticism when you least expected it. She loved catching people in their weakest moments. She was the person who kicked you when you were down. I stopped going to their family get-togethers because she attacked us girls every time. After my family and I moved to Minnesota, we didn't have to see her often. Thank goodness.

Wayne and Wanda came to visit sometimes. Wayne stayed quiet and kept the conversation superficial. I'm sure he didn't dare speak openly because Wanda was abusive toward him as well. He was a kind person and cared for the kids. When they visited, they sat and shared gossip, giving us all the news about everyone back home. Wanda became an elder at her church and shared with us gossip about some parishioners who foolishly believed they could trust her.

Dale said I made him feel like he was walking on eggshells. With his ongoing lying, theft, and porn use, I'm sure he was always afraid of being caught, which is why he felt that way. I'd feel the same if I engaged in those harmful and deceitful behaviors.

I stayed married to Dale for a long, miserable 23 years. He ran off with a new girlfriend, leaving me with a vehicle that had a ruined transmission. He married her as soon as our divorce became finalized. She can have him. I was relieved to be done with him. Being in an abusive relationship and suffering even more trauma made it difficult for me to heal from the massive childhood traumas I had endured.

Dale received his karma with his new wife. She has a gambling addiction, so now he gets to experience what it's like to be stolen from all the time. She also has histrionic personality disorder, which means she flirts with and makes moves on any man or young boy nearby. Dale is now experiencing how it feels to be cheated on. The grass isn't greener on the other side of the fence. He didn't realize that we make our grass green by watering the grass we already have. That works great every time.

After I divorced Dale, I started dating again, but I kept running into a lot of *broken toasters!* All they offered was a bunch of burnt toast! After trying the dating scene for a while, I decided to stay single. It was time to work on myself. I had to focus on healing from a lifetime of trauma and abuse. I needed to flip all of my Scrambled Eggs to Sunny Side Up.

I had to figure out how to prevent harmful people from entering my life. I wasn't sure how I was going to do that. One thing I knew was that I had to build a wall of assertive protection around myself. I also knew I had to become my own best friend. I needed to focus on loving myself because if I didn't, who would? Thankfully, my story has a happy ending. However, that's another story for another time, which I'll share with you in my next book — "Sunny Side Up, Eggshells to Seashells." See you there!

www.ingramcontent.com/pod-product-compliance
Lightning Source LLC
LaVergne TN
LVHW010917110826
845149LV00013B/2402
9798994620083